THE ROYAL NAVY 1914 - 1918
A PHOTOGRAPHIC RECORD

Adrian Vicary

The 5th Battle Squadron on a North Sea sweep in late 1917 or early 1918. HMS *Barham*, leading, has her kite balloon aloft. The weather conditions would have been at the limit for the balloon to be in the air; if the crew were in the basket it would have been an extremely uncomfortable experience. Following in the line is *Malaya*, then *Valiant* and *Warspite*, whose A and B turrets are in the foreground. Note fore-turrets trained to starboard to keep the guns out of the spray-laden wind. *Warspite*'s B turret displays the deflection scale to indicate to the next ship ahead the training angle when engaging a target. *Valiant*'s X turret is similarly marked. The second half of this system was the range clock, a clock-like face with a single pointer which would show the target range in thousands of yards. Two pairs of these can be seen on the corners of the searchlight platform behind *Valiant*'s aft funnel. Similar clocks were carried on the foremast.

INTRODUCTION

The photographs presented here are from negatives and prints in the collection of my father, the late Philip Vicary. They originate from a number of different photographers whose names have been recorded, together with some from the inevitable "unknowns". Many are from the naval photograph part of the collection founded by F. C. Bowen and F. C. Poyser in about 1925, operating as the Nautical Photo Agency in London and, latterly, Beccles. The driving force of the NPA, as far as the handling of the negatives and the production of prints were concerned, was Frederick Poyser, and after his death in 1960 these negatives were given to P. A. Vicary and became part of his Maritime Photo Library, the name created for the collection in around 1966.

Original photographers known were: M. Adam, G. C. Adams, H. E. Musson, H. Pank, F. C. Poyser, L. Sealy, Captain Thompson and H. L. Vicary. The following, sometimes only recorded by surname, may simply have supplied the negative or print from an unknown origin: Captain Borrisow, F. C. Bowen, J. David, G. F. Donaldson, Captain Downton, Holberton, Lister and L. Rust.

The aim is to present as broad a picture as possible of the many different types and classes from battleships to auxiliaries. It is obviously not possible to illustrate every class but a wide variety is shown. The arrangement is chronological as much as possible by the date of the individual photographs, which means that classes will not necessarily be in the right order. However, the building dates given in the ships' data notes will help to indicate the design progression. The notes given concentrate on the operational career of the particular ship pictured and these vary in length depending on the occurrence of highlights during their service. I make no apology for the inclusion of several ships where the notes are short - they, and their ship's companies, all played their part in the conflict and, as is always the case, some were simply not in the right (or wrong) place to achieve undying fame. Similarly, some photographs which might be considered technically sub-standard are included because they have a rarity interest and have not been seen in print for many years, if at all.

While the aim here is to present a collection of photographs of ships and give some idea of the wide-ranging involvement of the Royal Navy in the Great War, there were important roles involving the Senior Service in the conflict on land, particularly deserving of mention being the Royal Naval Air Service Squadrons, which provided considerable support to the Royal Flying Corps on the Western Front. These units had some of the leading fighter pilots and the best aircraft on the Allied side, particularly the great series from Sopwith - Pup, Triplane and Camel. There were also significant developments in strategic bombing.

Adrian Vicary
Cromer, 2014

First published in the United Kingdom in 2014 by Maritime Books, Lodge Hill, Liskeard, Cornwall, PL14 4EL

*HMS **Valiant** (nearest) and **Warspite** of the 5th Battle Squadron in late 1917 or early 1918.*

Note: Regarding the ships' data in the following pages -

• Requisitioned merchant ships are mostly recorded by their gross tonnage rather than displacement. Gross tonnage was a measurement of the ship's total enclosed volume including accommodation, cargo and machinery spaces, fuel tanks and bunkers etc. One gross ton = 100 cubic feet. There is no ratio or formula for conversion to displacement (1 ton = 2,240 lbs) which was always the greater as can be seen from the few examples where the two figures are available (eg: *Engadine*).

• Length is always the overall figure except where noted (pp) which means between perpendiculars. This is the longitudinal measurement between vertical lines through the centre of the anchor hawse-pipe and the rudder post. Overall length was greater, say 20ft, depending on the size of the vessel and shape of the bow and stern.

• Armour thickness is given as maximum and minimum. In a capital ship there was a multitude of different thicknesses used over various compartments, thickest at the most vulnerable points eg: magazines and engines. The belt, or side, armour could be vertical or inclined and the deck, horizontal or sloping.

Caroline Class Light Cruiser

Cammell Laird & Co. Ltd, Birkenhead
Laid down: 28th January 1914; Launched: 29th September 1914; Completed: December 1914
Displacement: 3,750 tons (Design); 4,219 tons (Load); 4,733 tons (FL)
Length: 446ft; Beam 41ft 6 in; Draught: 16ft
Power: Four-shaft Parsons Turbines; 40,000 shp - 28½ kts
Eight Yarrow boilers
Armament: 2 x 6-inch; 8 x 4-inch; 1 x 13-pdr AA; 4 x 21-inch Torpedo Tubes
Armour: Belt 3-1 inch; Deck 1-inch; Conning Tower 6-inch
Complement: 300

Still in builder's hands and flying the Red Ensign, HMS *Caroline* running full power trials in the Autumn of 1914. In December that year she joined the Grand Fleet as leader of the 4th Destroyer Flotilla and then transferred to the 1st Light Cruiser Squadron in February 1915. Early in 1916 she went to the 4th LCS and was at the Battle of Jutland. She remained with the 4th LCS until after the Armistice and went with them to the East Indies in June 1919. She returned home and was paid off into dockyard control in February 1922. In 1924 she became the Harbour Training Ship for the Ulster Division RNVR at Belfast. During 1939-45 she served as the administrative centre for Londonderry based escorts and at the war's end was returned to the RNVR. Refitted by Harland and Wolff in 1951, she continued in the same role until 2011 and was then saved for preservation and restoration to her wartime appearance.

Arethusa Class Light Cruiser

Vickers Ltd, Barrow-in-Furness
Laid down: 12 March 1913; Launched: 21 October 1914; Completed: February 1915
Displacement: 3,500 tons (Design); 3,750 tons (Load); 4,400 tons (FL)
Length: 436ft; Beam 39ft; Draught: 13ft 6in
Power: Four-shaft Parsons Turbines; 40,000 shp - 28½ kts; Eight boilers
Armament: 2 x 6-inch; 6 x 4-inch; 1 x 3-pdr AA; 4 x 21-inch Torpedo Tubes
Armour: Belt 3 - 1 inch; Deck 1 inch

In contrast to **Caroline**, **Phaeton** is also shown while on trials and with a somewhat scruffy look, flying a Red Ensign four times the area of the White! She was completed in February 1915 and joined the 4th LCS, Grand Fleet but only for two months, as she was sent to the Dardanelles until September. On her return she joined the 1st LCS. She and her sister, **Galatea**, shot down Zeppelin **L7** on 4 May 1916. Twenty-seven days later the same pair fired the opening shots of the Battle of Jutland. In August 1917 she was converted to lay 74 mines; by March 1918 she had laid a total of 358 mines in five trips, including one to the Kattegat. Then back to the Grand Fleet with the 7th LCS. Postwar she transferred to the 2nd LCS with the Harwich Force and was in the Baltic operations. In February 1920 she started a twelve month refit, only to go into Reserve at Devonport and then be placed on the disposal list in May 1922 and sold for breaking up in January 1923.

Sharpshooter Class Torpedo-Gunboat

H.M. Dockyard, Chatham
Laid down: 4th July 1888; Launched: 30th April 1889; Completed: July 1891
Displacement: 735 tons (Design); 828 tons (Load); 1,070 tons (FL)
Length: 242ft; Beam: 27ft; Draught: 10ft 6in
Power: Two-shaft Triple Expansion engines; 2,500 ihp - 16½ kts
Two boilers
Armament: 2 x 4.7-inch; 4 x 3-pdr AA; 5 x 14-inch Torpedo Tubes
(three reloads carried)
Complement: 91

A notable lesson from the Russo-Japanese War, 1904-5, was the effectiveness of mines in crippling or sinking any size of warship. In the Royal Navy, steps were taken to provide the beginnings of a minesweeping capability by fitting out older small warships with sweeping gear. These were obsolete torpedo-gunboats and this, **Skipjack**, is one of them, converted in 1909 with gallows, winch and kite, and seen here in about 1913. At the outbreak of war she was Leader for Fleet Sweepers with the Grand Fleet. By mid-war she was with the 2nd Minesweeping Flotilla and by November 1918 was based at Oban with the 13th Flotilla. In February 1920 she was sold to breakers.

Alarm Class Torpedo-Gunboat

H.M. Dockyard, Sheerness
Laid down: 25 June 1891; Launched: 13 September 1892; Completed: November 1893
Displacement: 810 tons (Normal)
Length: 230ft (pp); Beam: 27ft; Draught: 12ft
Power: Two-shaft Triple Expansion engines; 3,500 ihp (forced draught) - 19 kts; Four boilers
Armament: 2 x 4.7-inch; 4 x 3-pdr AA; 5 x 14-inch Torpedo Tubes (three reloads carried)
Complement: 91

HMS *Leda*, another, slightly younger torpedo-gunboat, also converted, is shown here at Lowestoft in the summer of 1914 dressed overall for what was to be the last port fishing festival for several years. By 1915 she was Leader, Minesweeping Gunboats, a duty she continued in 1916. She, too, ended the war with the 13th Flotilla and went for breaking in July 1920.

Workman, Clark & Co.Ltd., Belfast for the Orient Steam Navigation Co.Ltd.
Launched: 27th March 1909.
12,128 gross tons.
Length: 535 ft 6 in; Beam; 64 ft; Draught; 38 ft 8 in.
Power: Two, four-cylinder, quadruple expansion engines; 14,000 ihp - 18 knots.
Armament: 8 x 4.7-inch; replaced in March 1915 by 8 x 6-inch.

One of the first large liners earmarked for use during war as armed merchant cruisers, Orient Line's *Otranto* began fitting-out promptly on 4th August 1914 and was ready only nine days later. After brief trials she was ordered to join Rear Admiral Sir Christopher Cradock's cruiser squadron to help search the South Atlantic for German commerce raiders off the east coast of South America. When information was received by the Admiralty that Vice Admiral von Spee's cruisers might be off the west coast, Cradock's ships proceeded through the Straits of Magellan and up the coast of Chile to look for them. What was about to happen was the first RN defeat in a naval engagement for a 100 years. At 1630 on 1st November, in clear conditions but with very rough seas, *Otranto* made the first sighting of the German ships. As she would be extremely vulnerable with no armour protection and only 4.7-inch guns, she was ordered to get away, as the armoured cruisers *Good Hope* and *Monmouth* and the light cruiser *Glasgow* formed into line. The outcome of what became known as the Battle of Coronel was the loss of both the armoured cruisers with no survivors including the squadron's commander. Only *Glasgow* escaped, damaged. *Otranto* returned home and continued to serve as an AMC, later in the war being used as a troopship. It was thus, while in a convoy and carrying American troops to Britain for the American Army on the Western Front, that, on 6th October 1918, she was in collision with another troopship, P&O's *Kashmir*. Not far from their destination in the Clyde but in rough conditions and taking in water, she attempted to anchor to transfer her troops to other ships but was driven ashore in Machir Bay on the west coast of the Isle of Islay and was wrecked. Eighty five of her crew were lost together with 346 soldiers.

Invincible Class Battlecruiser

Sir W.G. Armstrong, Whitworth & Co.Ltd., Elswick
Laid down: 2nd April 1906; Launched: 13th April 1907; Completed; March 1908
Displacement: 17,420 tons (normal); 20,135 tons (Full Load)
Length: 567 ft; Beam: 78 ft 8 in; Mean Draught: 26 ft.
Power: Four-shaft Parsons Turbines; 41,000 shp - 25 knots. 31 Yarrow boilers.
Coal: 1,000 tons (norm), 3084 tons (max.). Oil; 710 - 725 tons.
Endurance; 3,050 nm at 22.3 knots; 6,210 at 10 knots.
Armament: 8 x 12-inch; 16 x 4-inch; 5 x 18-inch torpedo tubes.
Armour: Belt: 6 - 4 inch; Deck: 2½ - ¾ inch; Turret: 7 inch; Barbette: 7 - 2 inch; Conning tower: 10 - 6 inch.
Complement: 799 orig., 1,032 in May 1916.

This famous photograph shows *Invincible* on 8th December 1914, at 22 knots, during the chase of von Spee's cruisers off the Falkland Islands. Her side bears the evidence of having been coaling when the enemy ships were sighted, as she had only arrived in Port William harbour (Port Stanley) the previous day.

On completing a refit, just before the outbreak of war, *Invincible* was ordered to Queenstown to guard against a German breakout, then went to the Humber to form the 2nd Battlecruiser Squadron with *New Zealand* and was at the Battle of Heligoland Bight on 28th August, supporting light forces. After the disaster at Coronel, she was ordered to the Falkland Islands as flagship of Vice Admiral Sir Frederick Doveton Sturdee, on 4th November. During the action she and her sister, *Inflexible*, sank the armoured cruisers *Scharnhorst* and *Gneisenau*, firing 513 and 661 12-inch shells respectively. *Invincible* was hit 22 times by return fire. On the way back to Britain she had a two-month refit at Gibraltar, With *Indomitable* and *Inflexible* she formed the 3rd BCS of the Battlecruiser Force at Rosyth. A refit in May 1916 preceeded a transfer to the Grand Fleet at Scapa Flow when the 5rd BCS replaced the 5th Battle Squadron, which went south to strengthen the BCF. She flew the flag of Rear Admiral the Hon. Horace Hood at the Battle of Jutland. On 31st May 1916 she disabled *Wiesbaden* and *Pillau* of the German 2nd Scouting Group and inflicted two serious hits on the Battlecruiser *Lützow*. Return fire from that ship and *Derfflinger* scored five hits on her, the last of which blew the roof off Q turret and set fire to cordite. The flash reached the magazine causing a massive explosion. When the smoke cleared, the ship was in two halves with only the bow and stem remaining visible above the surface. Six survivors were picked up.

Chatham Class Light Cruiser

London & Glasgow Co.Ltd., Glasgow
Laid down: 11th February 1911; Launched: 29th August 1912; Completed; June 1913

(for ship's data, see *Melbourne* page 133)

Commerce raiders of the German Navy usually carried out their work acting alone to allow their commanders freedom of movement and to spread the few ships available as widely around the globe as possible. The light cruiser *Emden* was in the Indian Ocean in August 1914 and in three months succeeded in sinking l6 British merchant ships plus the Russian cruiser *Zhemtchug* and the French destroyer *Mousquet*. She also destroyed oil storage tanks at Madras and bombarded Penang. In the Cocos-Keeling Island group, on Direction Island, was the important cable and W/T station providing communications between Australia and England. In November Commander von Muller took *Emden* there to sever that link. News of the attack was received when *Sydney* was only 52 miles away, escorting an ANZAC convoy, and she was immediately diverted there. On 9th November she engaged and sank *Emden* being only slightly damaged by return fire. In December 1914 she was sent to the North America and West Indies Station until 1916 and then joined the 2nd Light Cruiser Squadron, Grand Fleet, with which she remained until the Armistice. She returned to Australia in March 1919 escorting the J-class submarines which had been presented to the Royal Australian Navy. She was RAN flagship from September 1924 to 1927, paid-off in 1928 and was broken up in 1929.

*HMS **Kent** coaling in Port William on 9th December 1914 after the chase of the German cruisers. Note the broken-off fore-topgallant mast which carried the wireless aerials.*

Kent Class Armoured Cruiser

H.M. Dockyard, Portsmouth
Laid down: 12th February 1900; Launched: 6th March 1901; Completed: October 1903
Displacement: 9,800 tons.
Length: 463 ft 6 in; Beam: 66 ft 0 in; Draught; 25 ft 0 in.
Power: Two four-cylinder triple expansion engines; 22,000 ihp - 23 knots.
31 Belleville boilers. Coal: 1,600 tons.
Armament: 14 x 6-inch; 10 x 12-pdr; 3 x 3 pdr; 2 x 18-inch torpedo tubes.
Armour: Belt 4 - 2 inch; Deck 2 - ¾ inch; Gunshield - 5 inch; Barbette - 5 inch; Conning Tower - 10 inch.
Complement: 678

When the war began she had recently completed a refit at Portsmouth; this was her first return to home waters having been on the China Station from 1906-1913. She was sent to the Falkland Islands in September 1914 and played an important part in the action on 8th December. Although not fully coaled, she was the first ship to leave harbour with orders to make a smoke-screen in an attempt to conceal the presence of the battlecruisers. During the chase she engaged *Leipzig* with her sister, *Cornwall*, together with *Glasgow* and then separated to chase *Nurnberg* alone. Reputedly, the boiler safety valves were screwed down to obtain every ounce of steam allowing her to reach 25 knots, never having made more than 22 before. *Nurnberg* burst two boilers and her speed reduced to 19 knots. *Kent* scored two hits during the chase but visibility was a problem because of the range and an increasing mist. ?the action lasted about two hours with the major part taking 50 minutes. She was hit 36 times herself, one shot knocking out the wireless room, and had much splinter damage. Ten survivors were picked up after *Nurnberg* sank but three died on board. As loss of her wireless left her unable to report the action, or her state, some concern about her fate was felt in the other ships until she returned. Her own concern was her fuel state owing to shortage of coal when she left harbour. Another story which emerged afterwards was that the situation was so desperate that stokers and crew searched for anything that would burn to feed the boiler furnaces, including the Chaplain's harmonium!

Four months later, on 14th March 1915 the *Dresden*, which had got away after the Falklands action, was found in the Juan Fernandez Islands, 600 miles off the coast of Chile, having run out of coal. After a short action with *Kent*, *Glasgow* and the AMC *Orama*, the German ship was sunk. *Kent* returned to the China Station then briefly home in May 1915. In 1916-1918 she was first in the Pacific and then at the Cape. Again briefly home in June, acting as a Channel convoy escort and then back to China in July. An unusual task for an RN ship in the East came in January 1919 when she went to Vladivostok during American and Japanese operations against the Bolsheviks. In March 1920 she was put on the Sale List in Hong Kong and went to the breakers in June.

Sir W.G. Armstrong, Whitworth & Co.Ltd., Elswick
Laid down as *Constitucion* for Chile: 26th February 1902; Launched: 12th January 1903;
Purchased for the Royal Navy and renamed: 3rd December 1903; Completed: June 1904
Displacement: 12,175 tons (Load)
Length: 479 ft 9 in; Beam: 71 ft 0 in; Draught: 25 ft 4 in.
Power: Two-shaft, three-cylinder, triple expansion engines; 12,500 ihp - 19 Knots
12 Yarrow boilers. Coal: 800 tons (norm); 2,000 tons (max).
Endurance: 6,250 nm at 10 knots.
Armament: 4 x 10-inch; 14 x 7.5-inch; 14 x 14-pdr; 2 x 12-pdr; 4 x 6-pdr;
2 x 18-inch torpedo tubes.
Armour: Belt 7 - 3 inch; Deck 3 - 1 inch; Turret 10 - 8 inch; Barbette 10 - 2 inch; Conning Tower 11 inch.
Complement: 802.

HMS *Swiftsure* is seen in the Suez Canal flying the flag of Vice Admiral R.H. Peirse, commanding the East Indies Station. She became flagship of the East Indies Squadron during 1913 and when war began, in August 1914, she began Red Sea patrols and escorted Indian troopships to Aden. From November 1914 she was flagship for forces defending the Suez Canal and fired on Turkish troops at Kantara. She was sent to the Dardanelles, arriving on 1st March 1915 and carried out the first of several successful bombardments on 2nd March. After the evacuation she returned home and was placed in reserve at Chatham. In 1917 all her armament was removed to prepare her for conversion to a blockship for an attack on the Belgian coast. This was to be a third attempt to block Ostend but the operation was cancelled. She was then used as an overflow accommodation ship. In 1919 she became a target ship and was sold for breaking up in June 1920.

Canopus Class Battleship

H.M. Dockyard, Devonport
Laid down: 15th February 1897; Launched: 5th July 1898; Completed: February 1900
Displacement: 12,950 tons (Design); 13,150 tons (Load); 14,300 tons (Deep load)
Length: 421 ft 6 in; Beam: 74 ft; Draught; 26 ft.
Power: Two-shaft, three-cylinder, triple expansion engines; 13,500 ihp - 18 knots
20 Belleville boilers. Coal: 800 tons (norm), 1,800 tons (max).
Endurance: 4,500 nm at 10 knots.
Armament: 4 x 12-inch; 12 x 6-inch; 12 x 12-pdr; 6 x 3-pdr; 4 x 18-inch torpedo tubes.
Armour: Belt 6 - 2 inch; Deck 2 - 1 inch; Turret 9 inch; Barbette 12 - 6 inch; Conning' Tower 12 inch.
Complement: 683

*HMS **Ocean** (right), also shown with the forces defending the Suez Canal in February 1915.*

Before the war *Ocean* was with the 4th Division, Home Fleet, from 1910 and in 1913-14 was stationed at Pembroke. By this time her best speed had dropped to about 13-15 knots. In August 1914 she joined the 8th Battle Squadron at Devonport and went to Queenstown. In September she was sent to the East Indies Squadron and took part in Persian Gulf operations in October. After being with the Suez Canal forces she was ordered to the Mediterranean and took part in the Dardanelles bombardments in February and March 1915. On 18 March at 1830 she was damaged by gunfire from the Turkish forts and then struck a floating mine while manoeuvring to take the crippled *Irresistible* in tow. She was abandoned about an hour after being first hit and sank three hours later.

Lord Nelson Class Battleship

William Beardmore & Co.Ltd., Dalmuir
Laid down: 15th May 1905; Launched: 23rd June 1906; Completed: June 1908
Displacement: 15,925 tons (Load); 17,683 tons (Deep load)
Length: 443 ft 6 in; Beam; 79 ft 6 in; Draught: 27 ft.
Power: Two-shaft, four-cylinder ,triple expansion engines; 16750 ihp - 18 knots
15 Yarrow boilers. Coal: 900 tons (norm), 2,171 tons (max);
Oil: 1,090 tons. Endurance: 9,180 nm at 10 knots.
Armament: 4 x 12-inch; 10 x 9.2-inch; 24 x 12-pdr; 10 x 3-pdr; 5 x 18-inch torpedo tubes.
Armour: Belt: 12 - 4 inch; Deck: 4 -1 inch; Main armament: Turret: 12 inch; Barbette: 12 - 3 inch;
9.2-inch gun houses: 8 - 7 inch; Conning tower: 12 inch.
Complement: c800.

*HMS **Agamemnon** (left) in camouflage during the Dardanelles campaign in 1915.*

Although building commenced five months before **Dreadnought** was laid down, that ship's design influenced this class of two ships. They were the ultimate in mixed-calibre gun battleship design, the type subsequently distinguished as Pre-Dreadnought battleships. She was with the 5th Battle Squadron, in the Channel after the outbreak of war, based at Portland. In February 1915 she and her sister, **Lord Nelson**, went to the Dardanelles. She was at the start of the attack on 19th February firing on the major Turkish batteries at the entrance at Sedd-el-Bahr on the western, European, shore and Kum Kale to the east, on the Asiatic shore. She also took part in the subsequent bombardments and was hit more than 50 times by return fire. After the evacuation she was on the Salonika Station and there, on 5 May 1916, she shot down the Zeppelin **LZ85**. (*Service career notes continued p.109*)

Most ships in the Royal Navy had a Mascot on board, very often a cat or dog, but **Agamemnon**'s was more unusual. It was a jackdaw. How the bird came to join the ship's company is not known but its very sad end was recorded by H.M. Denham in his book '*Dardanelles - A Midshipman's Diary*'. During the morning, of 18 October 1915 the bird was flying round the ship, when at sea, but a gust of wind blew him a long way astern.. Although the bird tried for a long time to fly back, exhaustion eventually made him flop into the sea where he died before the steam-cutter could effect a rescue.

*With a dark panel on her hull and two-tone striping on her funnels, HMS **Tiger** is shown back in Scottish waters on 29th January 1915, five days after the Dogger Bank action.*

John Brown & Co. Ltd., Clydebank
Laid down: 20th June 1912; Launched: 15th December 1913; Completed: October 1914
Displacement: 28,500 tons (Design); 32,800 tons (Load); 33,677 tons (Full Load)
Length; 704 ft 0 in; Beam; 90 ft 6 in; Mean Draught: 28 ft 5 in.
Power: Four-shaft Brown-Curtis Turbines; 108,000 shp - 29 Knots.
39 Babcock & Wilcox Boilers. Coal: 450 tons (min.), 3,320 tons (max.);
Oil; 450 tons (min); 3,480 tons (max). Endurance: 2,800 nm at 25 knots; 5,200 at 12.
Armament: 8 x 13.5-inch; 12 x 6-inch; 4 x 3-pdr; 2 x 3-inch AA guns; 4 x 21-inch torpedo tubes.
Armour: Belt 9 - 3 inch; Deck 3 - 1 inch; Turret 9 - 1 inch; Barbette 9 - 1 inch; Conning Tower 10 - 3 inch
Complement: 1,112 in 1914; 1,459 in 1918.

She joined the 1st Battlecruiser Squadron, Grand Fleet, on 6th November 1914 and was with the battlecruisers providing distant cover for a seaplane carrier raid on Cuxhaven on 25 December 1914. She received heavy damage passing through a severe storm on returning to Rosyth. At Dogger Bank on 24 January 1915 she received six hits and at Jutland she was hit 15 times, with two turrets out of action for some time. Repairs at Rosyth took a month. Postwar she served in the Atlantic Fleet BCS until 1922. After a refit she became a seagoing gunnery training ship in 1924-29. She then returned, to the Atlantic Fleet until 1931 when she finally paid-off at Devonport in May. She was sold to breakers in February 1932.

*HM Submarine **AE2** seen in the Suez Canal in February 1915.*

E-class Submarine, First Group

Vickers Ltd., Barrow-in-Furness
Launched: 22nd May 1913
Displacement: 655 tons (surface), 796 tons (submerged)
Length: 178 ft 1 in; Beam; 22 ft 8 in; Draught: 12 ft 0 in.
Power: Two-shaft, eight-cylinder, diesel engines; 1,600 hp - 15 knots;
two electric motors; 840 hp - 9 knots (submerged). Fuel: 45 tons.
Range: 3,000 nm at 10 knots on the surface.
Armament: 4 x 18-inch torpedo tubes (8 torpedoes carried); 1 x 12-pdr.
Complement: 30.

She was the second of two E-cass submarines built for the Royal Australian Navy. Both boats, when completed, were sent out to Singapore early in 1914, escorted by the cruiser ***Eclipse***. She went to the Mediterranean in March 1915 and was the first submarine to pass through the nets and minefields of the Dardanelles to reach the Sea of Marmora on 25 April. Only five days later she was badly damaged by gunfire from the Turkish torpedo-boat ***Sultanhisar*** and had to be scuttled.

*HMS **Carnarvon** at Quebec, discharging ammunition before drydocking at Montreal, May 1915.*

Devonshire Class Armoured Cruiser

William Beardmore & Co. Ltd., Dalmuir
Laid down: 1st October 1902; Launched: 7th October 1903; Completed: May 1905
Displacement: 10,850 tons (Load)
Length: 473 ft 6 in; Beam: 68 ft 6 in; Draught 24 ft.
Power: Two-shaft, four-cylinder, triple expansion, engines; 21,000 ihp - 22 knots
17 Niclausse boilers (the class was given different boilers to test the various designs available - six ships - four different types of boiler); Coal: 1,950 tons.
Armament: 4 x 7.5-inch; 6 x 6-inch; 2 x 12-pdr; 18 x 3-pdr; 2 x 18-inch torpedo tubes.
Armour: Belt 6 - 2 inch; Deck 2 - ¾ inch; Turret 5 inch; Barbette 6 inch; Conning tower: 12 inch
Complement: 655.

From March 1912 she was in the 2nd Fleet at Devonport and was flagship of the 5th Cruiser Squadron to the outbreak of war. She then went overseas and did not return home until the Armistice. In August 1914 she went to Cape Verde and captured a German merchantman on the 24th. To Montevideo in October 1914. At the Battle of the Falklands she led the cruisers and joined the battlecruisers in pounding ***Gneisenau***. From March 1915 to November 1918 she was on the North America & West Indies Station. She tore out some bottom plating on a shoal near the Abrolhos Rocks in February 1916 and put in for repairs at Rio de Janeiro. When she returned home she became a cadets' training ship in 1919. Put on the sale list in March 1921, she was sold for breaking up in November.

In order to provide extra 'Capital Ships', for example as escorts for merchant ships or troopships, where none could be spared, 14 merchant vessels were converted with dummy upperworks to give the appearance of various different classes of battleship or battlecruiser. The 8,360 gross ton *Montezuma*, launched in 1899 for the Canadian Pacific Railway Co., was hired on 2nd November 1914 for one of the conversions, becoming Dummy Battleship No3, representing *Iron Duke*. The additions were mainly built of wood but the result was convincing - the only give-away being the high freeboard of the mercantile hull. This would not be noticeable from any distance and might well deter a potential attacker. However the scheme did not last long and when one was sunk and the wooden turrets were seen floating away, the ruse was revealed. *Montezuma* was subsequently purchased on 7th July 1915 and became the naval oiler *Abadol*.

*HMS **Endymion** seen in drydock at Malta in 1915.*

Edgar Class Cruiser

Earle's Shipbuilding & Engineering Co. Ltd., Hull
Laid down: 21st November 1889; Launched: 22nd July 1891; Completed: May 1894
Displacement: 7,350 tons (Load)
Length: 387 ft 6 in; Beam: 60 ft; Draught; 23 ft 9 in.
Power: Two-shaft triple-expansion engines; 12,000 ihp (forced draught) - 20 knots.
Four double-ended cylindrical boilers.
Armament: 2 x 9.2-inch; 10 x 6-inch; 12 x 6-pdr; 5 x 3-pdr; 4 x 18-inch torpedo tubes.
Armour: Deck 5 - 3 inch; 9.2-inch Gunshields 3 inch; Conning Tower 12 inch.
Complement: 544

From August 1914 to February 1915 she was in the 10th Cruiser Squadron on the Northern Patrol. The old cruisers forming the squadron proved vulnerable to the severe weather conditions of the northern waters so they were paid-off. *Endymion* was one of the ships to have her two 9.2-inch guns and mountings removed for fitting in M15 class monitors. She received two further six-inch guns instead, giving a total of 12 of that calibre. Large anti-torpedo bulges were fitted and bow mounted net-sweeping gallows, as shown in the photograph. She, and two similarly equipped sisters were to serve as bombarding ships in the Dardanelles, where *Endymion* arrived in mid-1915. She remained in the Mediterranean, and in the Aegean in 1918, until the Armistice. She returned to the Nore and was paid-off in 1920 and sold for breaking up in March.

*HMS **Mersey** is seen on the beach at Zanzibar for bottom cleaning*

Vickers Ltd, Barrow-in-Furness
Laid down: 24th August 1912; Launched: 30th September 1913; Completed: February 1914
(see notes for ***Humber*** page 116)

She was one of the Brazilian river monitors and was to be named ***Madeira***. She commissioned for the Royal Navy in August 1914 and operated off the Belgian coast until November. After a refit at Chatham she was towed to Malta in March-April 1915 and then diverted, with sister ship ***Severn***, for the ***Konigsberg*** operations in East Africa. In a long and convoluted saga in which the German cruiser was trapped in the Rufiji river delta channels, but impossible to approach, it was the two monitors which provided the answer. Their shallow draught enabled them to enter the delta on 6th July 1915 at about 0600. Fired on by guns on shore as they moved upstream, they anchored below the islands behind which the German ship lay. Heavy fire from the cruiser scored hits, one knocking out ***Mersey***'s forward 6-inch gun so she shifted position and then retired to assess damage. Four men had been killed and three severely wounded, two of whom later died. ***Severn*** scored a hit with the aid of an RNAS aircraft spotter. ***Mersey*** came up again and also scored a hit with her after gun. Both monitors retired in the afternoon after signalling broke down with the aircraft. They returned on 11th July. Each ship fired in succession to avoid confusion to the aircraft spotting fall of shot. Hits were scored by ***Severn*** but the spotter was hit and its engine damaged. A short time later the engine failed and it had to ditch near ***Mersey*** who picked up both crew members. ***Severn*** kept firing and there was an explosion in ***Konigsberg*** and she stopped firing. ***Mersey*** then closed up to 7000 yards in range and with spotting from another aircraft, brought the cruiser to silence. ***Mersey*** remained in African waters with a refit at Durban in March 1916 and was then towed back to the Mediterranean in March-May 1918. She was at Mudros in October 1918 and went into the Black Sea and Danube after the Armistice. She returned to Devonport in May 1919, paid off into care and maintenance and moved to Queenstown in July. She was sold for breaking up in May 1921.

Motor Launches – First Group, numbers 1-50

Displacement: 34 tons.
Length: 75ft 0in; Beam: 12ft 0in; Draught: 4ft 0in
Second Group, numbers 51-550 and Third Group, numbers 551-580
37 tons. Length: 80ft 0in; Beam: 12ft 3in; Draught: 4ft 0in
Power: Two-shaft, six cylinder petrol engines: 440 bhp - 19 knots
Armament: 1 x 13-pdr (originally), 1 x 3-pdr (later), Depth charges.
Complement: 8

By 1915 the need for more small motor craft for inshore duties was apparent. As there was no spare capacity at U.K boat builders to do the work, the Admiralty sought a solution in America. On 9th April 1915 Canadian Vickers acting on the Admiralty's behalf, placed an order with Elco in Bayonne, New Jersey, for 50 motor launches. These wooden craft were constructed by Elco and sent as sets of parts to Canada where they were assembled at Montreal. The first 50 had a length of 75 feet but the second order placed on 8th June 1915, was for a further 500 boats with length increased to 80 feet. The intended armament was to be army 13 pounders, but these were subsequently required for arming merchant ships, so 3 pounders were fitted instead. When the boats arrived in Britain they were used to form six-boat ML patrol units manned by RNVR personnel. They were an improvement over the motorboats pressed into service earlier and despite the tendency of their petrol engines to overheat and catch fire, the large number available outweighed any disadvantages. Alleviation of the fuel problem was provided in 1916 by using a mixture of one part petrol to two parts paraffin. In July 1917 came a third and final order for 30 more 80-footers and the last had been delivered by February 1918. Their duties were many, including use as scouts, anti-submarine craft, inshore mine-sweeping, smokescreen genera- tors and hydrophone vessels.

*The first batch of M.L.s being loaded aboard **Statesman** at Montreal on 31 August 1915*

Statesman

Workman Clark & Co.Ltd., Belfast for T & J Harrison of Liverpool
Launched: 25th May 1895
6,322 gross tons
Length: 450ft 0in; Beam: 52ft 6in; Draught: 33ft 8in

Requisitioned as a transport on 4th August 1914. Damaged by torpedo from ***UB-43*** in the Mediterranean on 3rd November 1916 and sank two days later.

Returning to Mudros, probably at the end of her first patrol on 14th September 1915. This was when her gun mounting, placed aft of the conning-tower and here obscured by crew sitting on the casing, had collapsed due to being caught and strained in the nets during passage up the Dardanelles.

E-Class Submarine, First Group

H.M. Dockyard, Chatham
Launched: 23rd November 1912
(for boats data notes see *AE 2* page 21)

E2 was at Harwich from the start of the war into 1915 and was then sent to the Mediterranean to join the RN's submarine campaign. She arrived in Malta in July, where the Dockyard fitted a 4-inch gun, and left for her first patrol in August entering the straits on 13th and reaching the sea of Marmora on 14th. She was soon in action and during her month's patrol she sank or damaged at least 20 dhows, a gunboat, a destroyer and a large transport. The patrol was only marred by the loss of her First Lieutenant, who went ashore on 7th September with explosives to damage a railway but failed to return. When the Dardanelles operations concluded, she stayed in the Mediterranean and carried out anti-submarine patrols, sometimes in company with a decoy vessel, an idea that did not bring much success. She never returned to home waters and was sold for breaking up at Malta in March 1921.

In Mediterranean or Aegean waters at an unknown date.

E-class submarine, Second Group

H.M. Dockyard, Chatham
Launched: 5th September 1914
Displacement: 667 tons (surface); 807 tons (submerged)
Length: 181ft 0in; Beam: 23ft 6in; Draught: 12ft 6in
Power: Two-shaft, eight-cylinder, diesel engines: 1,600 hp - 15 knots
Two electric motors: 840 hp - 9 knots (submerged)
Armament: 5 x 18-inch torpedo tubes (10 torpedoes carried);
1 x 12-pdr. (replaced by 1 x 4-inch at Malta Dockyard)
Complement: 30

Also at Harwich with the 8th Submarine Flotilla, she was one of the boats involved in the Cuxhaven seaplane-carrier raid on 25th December 1914. She left for the Mediterranean in May 1915 and started her first patrol to the Sea of Marmora in June and her second in September during which she sank several Turkish merchant vessels. From 1916-18 she also took part in the patrols to counter the increasing U-boat presence in the Mediterranean and, like *E2*, was sold to breakers in Malta in 1921.

During the Gallipoli operations, embarking Field Marshal Lord Kitchener from the steam picket-boat alongside. Beyond is the battleship **Cornwallis**.

Beagle Class Destroyer (from 1913 designated the G-class)

John Brown & Co Ltd., Clydebank
Laid down: 1st April 1909; Launched: 11th December 1909; Completed: September 1910
Displacement: 953 tons (normal); c.1,100 tons (full load)
Length: 278ft 0in Beam: 27ft 6in Draught: 8ft 6in
Power: Three-shaft Parsons turbines; 14,300 shp - 27 knots. 5 Yarrow boilers.
Coal: c.220 tons Endurance: 1,530 nm at 15 knots.
Armament: 1 x 4-inch 3 x 12-pdr (designed for 5 x 12-pdr); 2 x 21-inch torpedo tubes (four torpedoes carried)
Complement: 96

She was in the Mediterranean with the 5th Destroyer Flotilla in August 1914, having been based there since 1911. When hostilities with Turkey began she was in the Gulf of Aqaba. In the Dardanelles campaign the Beagle class destroyers were used temporarily as minesweepers. In the landings at Anzac Cove on 24th April 1915, *Foxhound* was one of seven destroyers which went in close to the shore to disembark troops and at the Suvla landings on 6th and 7th August, she was again one of seven destroyers carrying 500 troops each and towing a 'beetle' with another 500 men. The 'beetles' were motor lighters, a primitive early type of shallow draught landing craft. She returned to home waters in late 1917 and served with the 2nd Destroyer Flotilla till the end of the war. She was sold for breaking up in November 1921.

At sea in about mid-1915 with a 3-inch AA gun on the searchlight platform on the aft superstructure.
The anti-torpedo nets and booms have been removed but were replaced for a time from late 1915 into 1916.

HMS Erin

Vickers Ltd, Barrow-in-Furness
Laid down: 6th December 1911; Launched 3rd September 1913; Completed: August 1914
Displacement: 22,780 tons (normal); 25,250 tons (full load)
Lenth: 559 ft 6 in; Beam: 91 ft 7 in; Draught: 28 ft 6 in (load), 30 ft 11 in (deep)
Power: Four-shaft Parsons turbines; 26,500 shp - 21 knots
15 Babcock and Wilcox boilers. Oil: 710 tons
Coal: 900 tons (norm.), 2,120 tons (max.)
Endurance: 5,300 nm at 10 knots on coal and oil;
3,400 nm at 10 knots using coal only.
Armament: 10 x 13.5-inch; 16 x 6-inch; 6 x 6-pdr (2 x 3-inch AA added during the war);
4 x 21-inch torpedo tubes.
Armour: Belt: 12 - 4 inch; Deck: 3 - 1 inch; Turret: 11 - 4 inch; Barbette: 10 - 3 inch;
Conning tower: 12 - 4 inch.
Complement: 976 (1914), 1,064 (1915)

She was being built for Turkey as **Rashadieh** (ex **Reshad V**) but was seized on the outbreak of war for the Royal Navy. She had a largely unremarkable war service starting with the 4th Battle Squadron, September 1914 - 1915, and then the 2nd Battle Squadron, Grand Fleet, 1915 - 18 and was present at Jutland. In March 1919 she was in the 3rd Battle Squadron, Home Fleet and then in October went into reserve at the Nore. From December 1919 to March 1920 she was a turret drill-ship at Chatham and then the flagship of the Nore Reserve with a refit at Devonport in July and August 1920. Placed on the disposal list in May 1922, she was sold for breaking up in December

Acacia Class Fleet Sweeping Sloop

William Simons & Co Ltd, Renfrew
Launched: 29 June 1915
Displacement: 1,200 tons
Length: 262ft 6in; Beam: 33ft; Draught: 11ft
Power: Single-shaft triple expansion engine; 1,800 ihp - 16½ knots; 2 Boilers
Coal: 130 tons (normal); 250 tons (max) Endurance: 2,000 nm at 15 knots
Armament: 2 x 12-pdr; 2 x 3-pdr AA
Complement: 90

On builder's trials in the summer of 1915 and clearly displaying her minesweeping gallows. Delivered to the Royal Navy on 17 July 1915, she became the Leader of the 1st Sloop Flotilla. Initially the Acacia group of the Flower class was used almost exclusively for minesweeping, as intended, but in 1917, when unrestricted U-boat warfare was announced and a convoy system for merchant ships introduced, they gave excellent service as escort vessels. Another ship with an apparently unremarkable career, she was sold in April 1923.

*In the eastern Mediterranean in September 1915 with a Short Type 166 seaplane from **Ark Royal** on board for spotting operations.*

Abercrombie Class Monitor

Swan, Hunter & Wigham Richardson, Wallsend on Tyne
Laid down: 17th December 1914; Launched: 15th April 1915; Completed: June 1915
Displacement: 6,150 tons (deep)
Length: 334 ft 6 in; Beam: (main hull) 60ft 0in, (over bulges) 90ft 2in; Draught: 10ft 0in.
Power: Two-shaft, three-cylinder, vertical triple expansion engines; 1,800 ihp - 6 knots,
2 x Babcock and Wilcox Boilers. Coal: 380 tons.
Endurance: 1,340 nm at 6 knots.
Armament: 2 x 14-inch; 2 x 12-pdr; 1 x 3-pdr; 1 x 2-pdr (2 x 6-inch added 1916-17)
(The 14-inch guns were American, originally for Greek battleships building in Germany)
Armour: Belt: 4 inch; Deck: 2 – 1 inch; Turret face: 10 inch; Barbette: 8 inch
Complement: 198

Commissioned in May 1915 and sent to the Dardanelles, she gave bombarding support for the Suvla Bay landings in August. She formed part of the 1st Division, Special Squadron, from September 1915 to January 1916. In the latter month she gave support for the evacuation of Cape Helles and returned home in February. After Zeppelin raids on East coast towns, she was sent to Great Yarmouth in May to act as guardship. She was docked on the Tyne in June 1917 and then went to the Thames estuary for planned Belgian landings which were not carried out. She returned to Yarmouth in October. She had a refit at Portsmouth in July 1918 and in 1919 she was paid-off into care & maintenance at Immingham. Although sold in May 1921 she was retained for Admiralty trials. In the 1930s these included trials of underwater protection for new construction. She was eventually sold for breaking up in September 1936.

TB91 Class Torpedo Boat

J. Samuel White & Co.Ltd., Cowes
Launched: 1894
Displacement: 130 tons
Length: 142 ft 3 in; Beam: 15 ft 3 in; Draught: 8 ft 9 in
Power: Triple expansion engine; 2,400 ihp - 23 knots. Coal: 21 tons
Endurance: 1,780 nm at 10 knots.
Armament: 3 x 3-pdr; 3 x 18-inch torpedo tubes (two reloads carried)
Complement: 18

An example of the old torpedo boat types still operating successfully for coastal duties, *TB96* was in the local defence flotilla at Gibraltar. She seems to have only one of her three torpedo tubes still mounted, that being aft of the mainmast. She otherwise has an extremely cluttered appearance, to say nothing of the washing drying anywhere convenient! When escorting to the east of Gibraltar in the early hours of 1st November 1915, she was sunk in collision with the troopship *Tringa*.

TB13-36 class Torpedo Boat (Coastal Destroyer)

J. Samuel White & Co.Ltd., Cowes
Laid down: 20th March 1907; Launched: 19th November 1907; Completed: May 1908
Displacement: 290 tons (full load)
Length: c.180 ft; Beam: 17 ft 6 in; Draught: 6 ft 0 in.
Power: Three-shaft parsons turbines; 3,750 shp - 26 Knots. Two Yarrow boilers.
Oil: 40 tons.
Armament: 2 x 12-pdr; 3 x 18-inch torpedo tubes
Complement: 35

She was one of the last series of Torpedo Boats, of larger dimensions, which were reclassified as Coastal Destroyers. Her war service was principally with the 6th Flotilla, Dover Patrol, from 1915 – 1918. She has a far smarter appearance with both guns and her three torpedo tubes clearly visible. She was sold in October 1920.

Workman Clark & Co.Ltd., Belfast for P&O
Launched: 1907
Length: 470 ft 3 in (pp); Beam: 56 ft 6 in.
8,089 gross tons.

The Royal Navy had a small number of hospital ships during the war operating under the Red Ensign. *Delta* was one of these for only a brief period from 5th August to 12th November 1914, after which she became a military hospital ship between 14th January 1915 and 19th March 1918. With accommodation for 530 patients, she was one of many used in the Gallipoli campaign in 1915-16.

Launched: 1902
466 gross tons.

A much smaller vessel was this very elegant steam yacht, presented for naval service by her owner, Admiral Sir David Beatty. She was a hospital ship at Rosyth throughout the war.

*HMS **Leonidas** (left) in the overall black livery worn by destroyers in 1915*

L class destroyer

Palmer's Shipbuilding & Iron Co., Hebburn on Tyne
Laid down: 26th October 1912; Launched: 30th October 1913; Completed: August 1914
Displacement: 987 tons (norm,), 1,150 tons (deep load)
Length: 268 ft 10 in; Beam: 27 ft 8 in; Draught: 10 ft 6 in.
Power: Two-shaft, Parsons all-geared turbines; 22,500 shp - 29 knots.
4 Yarrow boilers. Oil: 240 tons. Endurance: 1,720 nm at 15 knots.
Armament: 3 x 4-inch; 1 x 2-pdr; 1 x 0.303 Maxim; 4 x 21-inch torpedo tubes.
Complement: 73

As a new ship she joined the 3rd Destroyer Flotilla at Harwich and was one of the seaplane carriers' escorts for the Cuxhaven raid. In this photograph a prominent feature is the triangular device on the foremast. Made of wooden baulks, its purpose was to provide a recognition feature to avoid misidentification when in action with enemy destroyers. Diamond and triangle, point uppermost, symbols were also used and periodically changed to prevent the enemy attempting to emulate them. In 1917, with the other L class destroyers, she carried out convoy escort duties in the Channel based at Devonport and Portsmouth. In May 1921 she was sold to breakers.

Admiralty M Class Destroyer

William Denny & Brothers, Dumbarton
Laid down: 27th October 1914; Launched: 20th June 1915; Completed: November 1915
For class details, see *Milbrook* (page 94) except for the following:
Displacement: 1,025 tons (norm.), 1,250 tons (deep load)
Power: Three-shaft Parsons turbines; 25,000 shp - 34 Knots.
Oil: 266 tons. Endurance: 2,100 nm at 15 knots.

Very little detail is available about her service but this photograph is included as it shows an interesting stage in the evolution of destroyer colours. She has a black hull and grey upperworks. The date is likely to be late 1915 or early 1916, her full pendant number being H2C at that time. The high cliffs suggest the northern coast of Scotland or Ireland. She was sold for breaking up in November 1921.

*Photographed from **Southampton** in January 1916*

Birmingham class Light Cruiser

H.M. Dockyard, Chatham
Laid down: 29th July 1912; Launched: 23rd April 1913; Completed: April 1914
Length: 457 ft 0 in; Beam: 50 ft 0 in; Draught: 16 ft 0 in.
Displacement: 5,440 tons (norm.), 6,040 tons (deep load)
Power: Four-shaft Parsons turbines; 25,000 shp - 25½ knots.
12 Yarrow boilers. Coal: 1,165 tons; Oil: 235 tons.
Endurance: 4,140 nm at 16 knots.
Armament: 9 x 6-inch; 1 x 3-inch AA; 4 x 3-pdr; 2 x 21-inch torpedo tubes.
Armour: Belt: 3 inch (2 inch on 1 inch plating); Deck: 1½ - 3/8 inch; Conning tower: 4 inch.
Complement: 480

As a new ship she joined the 1st Light Cruiser Squadron and, in August 1914, sank a German merchant ship. On 28th of that month she was at the Heligoland Bight action and, in January 1915, she was present at the Battle of Dogger Bank. In February she joined the 2nd Light Cruiser Squadron as flagship. In 1916 she went out to the Mediterranean as flagship of the 8th Light Cruiser Squadron, which, in the final year of the war was part of the Adriatic Force. Her postwar service was all on foreign stations, starting with the 6th Light Cruiser Squadron, Africa Station, of which she was flagship from August 1921 until 1924. She was eventually sold for breaking up in January 1931.

*(Left) Submarine Scout airship, believed to be **SS3**, known as 'Silver Queen' at Mudros, over the cruiser **Lowestoft** in 1916.*

SS Airship (BE2c Type)

Crew of 2 – pilot with W/T operator in front cockpit.
Length: 143 ft 5 in; Max. diameter: 27 ft 9 in;
Height (top of envelope to skids): 43ft 5in.
Envelope capacity: 60,000 cu.ft. of hydrogen
Engine: 70/75 hp eight-cylinder Renault, air-cooled. 60 gallons of petrol.
4-blade propeller; Max.speed: c.50mph. Climb rate: 700ft/min.
Operational height: Up to 4,000ft.
Endurance: at full speed: 7-8 hours; at half-throttle: 14-16 hours.
Weapons load: 8 x 16lb bombs on fuselage rack; 2 x 65lb bombs below pilot's seat.

Developed by the Royal Naval Air Service at Kingsnorth constructional and experimental airship station in Kent in the early months of 1915, the prototype made use of materials from an earlier airship, stored at Farnborough, together with a BE2c aeroplane fuselage. Commissioned on 18th March as **SS1**, trials were successful and the design was contracted out for production. In the Dardanelles campaign a small group, consisting of **SS3**, **SS7**, **SS8**, **SS17** and **SS19**, formed the Airship Expeditionary Force. The unit's main duties were anti-submarine convoy duty and photographic reconnaissance. They also did mine-spotting and, occasionally, artillery spotting. The SS series and subsequent types of airship played an essential part in the anti-submarine, mine-spotting and shipping escort tasks carried out from the numerous coastal bases around the British Isles.

Acasta Class Destroyer (K class from 1913)

John Brown & Co.Ltd., Clydebank
Laid down: 15th January 1912; Launched: 14th November 1912; Completed: March 1913
Displacement: 935 tons (norm.); 1,072 tons (deep load)
Length: 267ft 6in; Beam: 27ft 0in; Draught: 9ft 6in.
Power: Two-shaft, Brown-Curtis turbines; 24,500 shp - 29 knots.
4 Yarrow boilers. Oil: 200 tons. Endurance: 1,540 nm at 15 knots.
Armament: 3 x 4-inch; 2 x 2l-inch torpedo tubes (four torpedos carried).
Complement: 73

On completion she joined the 4th Destroyer Flotilla which became part of the Grand Fleet from August 1914. At Jutland, she fired torpedoes in the night action with German cruisers and destroyers. In the late summer of 1916 the flotilla moved to the Humber, then to Portsmouth at the end of the year. In spring 1917 she was based at Devonport. She was sold for breaking up in May 1921.

Fairfield Shipbuilding & Engineering Co.Ltd., Govan, Glasgow
Laid down: 1913; Launched: 30th June 1915
14,744 gross tons.
Length: 550 ft 0 in; Beam: 65 ft 10 in.
Power: Two-shaft, geared turbines; 16,000 shp - 18 knots.
Armament: 8 x 6-inch; 2 x 6-pdr.

A new ship, building for the Union Steamship Co. of New Zealand as *Aotearoa*, she was taken over by the Admiralty on 21st June 1915 and completed as an Armed Merchant Cruiser. She was commissioned in December for service with the 10th Cruiser Squadron in northern waters. On 14th June 1917 she was returning from a patrol north-west of the Shetland Islands to Scapa Flow to refuel. At just after 2.00 am , a single torpedo, fired by *U-69*, hit her. As the day wore on flooding increased and she was abandoned, all but one of her crew being safely transferred to other vessels. She finally sank about 10 hours after being first hit.

Cook, Welton & Gemmell, Beverley, for the Onward Steam Fishing Co., Grimsby
Launched: 1913
202 gross tons.
Armament: 1 x 6-pdr

This trawler is included as a typical example of the hundreds hired for naval service. Many, including **Libyan**, were used for minesweeping and others for patrol duties, on the watch for prowling U-boats. As the loss details show, hired trawlers were the most vulnerable ships in the fleet; accounts are many of their succumbing to mines, often breaking up with great rapidity and with few, if any, survivors. **Libyan** survived the war, in service from February 1915 to 1919, went back to fishing and returned to serve in the Second World War.

On the way to Hoyer with Harwich Force destroyers escorting

Sir W.G. Armstrong, Whitworth & Co.Ltd., Low Walker
Laid down: 1904; Launched: 7th March 1905; Completed: May 1907
Displacement: 2,950 tons (1,951 gross tons)
Length: 361 ft 0 in; Beam: 42 ft 0 in; Draught: 16 ft 0 in (max.)
Power: Three-shaft Parsons turbines; 11,000 shp - 23 knots. 4 boilers.
Coal: 475 tons. Endurance: 995 nm at 10 knots.
Armament: 4 x 12-pdr; 1 x 6-pdr AA.
Aircraft: Two landplanes in forward hangar - launching platform 64 ft x 25 ft max. Five aeroplanes in aft hangar.
Complement: 218

She was the Isle of Man Steam Packet Co's *Viking*, taken over on 15th March 1915 for conversion to a seaplane carrier by Cunard at Liverpool, commissioned in September and purchased outright in October. Operating from the Nore and Harwich, she was to have an eventful naval career, beginning with the first carrier take-off by a landplane. This was on 3rd November 1915 when Flt.Lt. B.F. Fowler flew Bristol Scout C No.1255 from her take-off deck forward and flew ashore to land. On 25th March 1916 five of *Vindex*'s seaplanes took off to attack Zeppelin sheds thought to be at Hoyer on the Schleswig coast, near the border with Denmark. The attempt was abortive, as three seaplanes were lost and the discovery made that there was no Zeppelin base at Hoyer. It was actually ten miles inland at Tondern. A further raid was attempted on 4th May, with *Engadine*, but again met with no success. More than two years would pass before better results would be achieved. On 2nd August 1916 Flt.Lt. C.T. Freeman, in Bristol Scout D No. 8953, flew off to attack the Zeppelin *L17*. Although again unsuccessful this was the first attempted interception by a carrier-based aeroplane. *Vindex* went to the Mediterranean in 1918 and saw out the last months of the war with nothing particular to note. She returned home to pay-off in late 1919 and was sold back to her owners in February 1920.

At Dunkirk in 1916

Torpedo Boat Destroyer, grouped in 1912 into the C-class of three-funnel 30-knotters.

Fairfield Shipbuilding & Engineering Co.Ltd,. Govan, Glasgow
Laid down: 24th January 1898; Launched: 28th June 1898; Completed: July 1899
Displacement: 370 tons (light); 420 tons (full load)
Length: 215 ft 6 in; Beam: 21 ft 0 in; Draught: 8 ft 2 in.
Power: Two-shaft, triple expansion engines; 6,300 ihp - 30 knots.
Thornycroft boilers. Coal 45 tons (min.), 85 tons (max.).
Endurance: 1,440 nm at 11 knots.
Armament: 1 x 12-pdr; 5 x 6-pdr; 2 x 18-inch torpedo tubes.
Complement: 63

Her entire wartime career was with the 6th Destroyer Flotilla, Dover Patrol. Much of this was on the vital task of escorting the endless to-and-fro of cross-channel passenger vessels and transports. On one such occasion, in the winter of 1915, her bows were badly damaged in a collision with a transport at night. In rough weather, the six-funnelled Tribal class destroyer *Viking* secured her alongside and slowly proceeded to Dover where a tug came out to tow both ships to a buoy in the harbour. Her greatest achievement, rare for any ship in this war and especially for an aged TBD, came on 26th January 1918. On a Channel Barrage patrol she sank the submarine *UB-35* with depth charges. She was sold in September 1920.

Tribal class destroyer, First group, F class from 1913

Sir W.G.Armstrong, Whitworth & Co.Ltd, Elswick
Laid down: 9th August 1906; Launched: 8th May 1907; Completed: September 1909
Displacement: 872 tons (norm.); 966 tons (deep load)
Length: 263 ft 6 in; Beam: 25 ft 0 in; Draught: 7 ft 6 in.
Power: Three-shaft Parsons turbines; 14,000 shp - 33 knots. 5 Yarrow boilers.
Oil: c.200 tons. Endurance: 1,400 nm at 15 knots.
Armament: 5 x 12-pdr; 2 x 18-inch torpedo tubes
In 1917: 2 x 4.7-inch; 1 x 2-pdr PomPom; 1 x Maxim machine-gun;
two depth-charge throwers; four DCs carried.
In 1918: 2 x 14-inch torpedo tubes at break of focsle for close-range action.
Complement: 68

Like **Leven**, this destroyer served from 1914 to 1918 with the 6th Destroyer Flotilla, Dover Patrol, on similar duties. During one of the cross-Channel escorting duties she went alongside the torpedoed London, Brighton & South Coast Railway steamer, **Sussex**, and rescued passengers. A notable incident in the anti-submarine war in the Dover Patrol's area of operations, came on 23/24th April 1916. The hired drifter, **Gleaner of the Sea**, equipped with mined anti-submarine nets, caught **UB-13** in her nets and disabled her with a hand-thrown lance bomb. Unable to do more, **Afridi** arrived to complete the job by firing her explosive sweep over the spot. She was sold in December 1919.

William Denny & Brothers, Dumbarton
Laid down: 1910; Launched: 23rd September 1911; Completed: 1912
Displacement: 2,550 tons (1,676 gross tons)
Length: 316 ft 0 in; Beam: 41 ft 0 in; Draught: 16 ft 0 in.
Power: Three-shaft Parsons turbines; 13,800 shp - 21½ knots.
6 Babcock & Wilcox boilers. Coal: 400 tons.
Armament: 2 x 4-inch; 1 x 6-pdr AA.
Aircraft: Four to Six seaplanes.
Complement: 197

A South Eastern & Chatham Railway steamer, requisitioned on 11th August 1914 and commissioned two days later, she was fitted-out at Chatham with canvas hangars for three aeroplanes. In this form, together with her sister, *Riviera*, and half-sister *Empress*, she took part in the first attempted ship-borne air raid. With two destroyers and ten submarines, the force set out to attack the Zeppelin base at Cuxhaven on 25th December 1914. Nine aircraft were hoisted out, of which seven successfully took off. However, the raid failed because of thick mist and an encounter with Zeppelins and German seaplanes. As was to become only too familiar, the intelligence was faulty and the airship base was at Nordholz, ten miles south of Cuxhaven. Only three aircraft returned to the ships but the other crews were picked up by the accompanying submarines. In 1915 *Engadine* was fitted with a permanent hangar, by Cunard, to house four seaplanes. She was then attached to the Battle Cruiser Force, Grand Fleet, from 1915 to 1917. At Jutland, one of her Short 184s sighted the High Seas Fleet, but the report failed to get through. In the action, the armoured cruiser *Warrior* was badly damaged by gunfire and taken in tow by *Engadine*. The cruiser slowly settled and sank the next day (1st June) but all 600 survivors were transferred to the carrier. In 1918 she went to Malta and was in the Mediterranean until 1919 when she returned home, and to her owners at the end of the year.

*With **Lion** off Rosyth, post-Jutland, in the period when **Lion** was without her Q turret.*

Lion Class Battlecruiser

Vickers Ltd., Barrow-in-Furness
Laid down: 2nd May 1910; Launched: 29th April 1911; Completed: November 1912
Displacement: 26,400 tons (norm.); 30,186 (deep load)
Length: 700 ft 0 in; Beam: 88 ft 6 in; Draught: 28 ft 10 in.
Power: Four-shaft Parsons turbines; 70,000shp - 27 knots. 42 Yarrow boilers.
Coal 1,000 tons (min.), 3,520 (max.). Oil: 1,135 tons.
Endurance: 5,610 nm at 10 knots.
Armament: 8 x 13.5-inch; 16 x 4-inch; 1 x 4-inch AA; 1 x 3-inch AA; 2 x 21-inch torpedo tubes.
Armour: Belt: 9-4 inch; Deck: 2-1 inch; Turret: Barbette: 9-3 inch; Conning tower: 10 inch.
Complement: c.1,100

In 1913 she was in the 1st Battle Cruiser Squadron which, on the outbreak of war, became part of the Grand Fleet. She was at the Heligoland Bight on 28th August and was detached to the West Indies to guard against possible attack by Von Spee's squadron. After the Falkland Islands, she returned to the 1st BCS early in 1915 and was at Dogger Bank on 24th January. When **Lion** became flagship of the Battle Cruiser Force, **Princess Royal** took over as Flagship of the squadron. At the Battle of Jutland she was hit nine times, but despite fires, her fighting ability was not impaired. She underwent refit in Portsmouth and returned to Rosyth on 21st July. In 1919 she was in the Atlantic Fleet and in 1920 she was placed in the Reserve Fleet at Rosyth. As with many other capital ships, under the terms of the Washington Naval Treaty, she was sold for breaking up in December 1922.

Lord Clive Class Monitor

Harland & Wolff, Belfast
Laid down: 9th January 1915;   Launched: 8th July 1915; Completed: August 1915
Displacement: 5,850 tons
Length: 335 ft 6 in; Beam: (main hull) 57 ft 0 in; (over bulges) 87 ft 2 in; Draught: 9 ft 7 in.
Power: Two-shaft, four cylinder, vertical triple expansion engines; 2,310 ihp - 6½ knots. 2 boilers.
Coal 356 tons. Endurance 1,100 nm at 6½ knots.
Armament: 2 x 12-inch; 2 x 12-pdr; 1 x 3-pdr AA; 1 x 2-pdr AA (4 x 6-inch added 1916/17)
Armour: Belt 6 inch; Deck 2 - 1 inch; Turret face 10½ inch; Barbette 8 inch;
Complement: 194

These monitors were given turrets from older pre-Dreadnought battleships, *General Craufurd*'s coming from *Magnificent*. She commissioned in August 1915 and joined the Monitor squadron at Dover. She was in many of the bombardments on the Belgian coast between 1915 and 1918 and, on several occasions during the period from July 1916 to April 1917 she embarked two Short 184s for spotting. In November 1918 she paid-off at Sheerness. She recommissioned as a gunnery tender to the 1st Fleet in January 1919. Later that year she was offered for sale to Romania, which came to nothing, and paid-off again and was placed on the sale list in spring 1920. She was sold for breaking up in May 1921.

In the Dover Patrol in 1916 with the forward 6-inch gun mounted.

Experimental Destroyer/Flotilla leader

Cammell Laird & Co.Ltd., Birkenhead
Laid down: 30th October 1906; Launched: 7th December 1907; Completed: February 1910
Displacement: 2,170 tons (norm.) 2,390 tons (deep load)
Length: 353 ft 9 in; Beam: 34 ft 2 in; Draught: 11ft 5 in (norm.), 12 ft 6½ in (deep)
Power: Four-shaft Parsons turbines; 30,000 shp - 35 knots. 12 Laird boilers.
Oil:192 tons (norm.), 282 tons (max.). Endurance: 2,335 nm at 15 knots.
Armament: 4 x 4-inch; 2 x 18-inch torpedo tubes.
Complement: 126

In 1912 she was Captain (D)'s ship in the 4th Destroyer Flotilla; as leader of the K class, she became part of the Grand Fleet in August 1914. The rough weather encountered in northern waters proved too great a strain on her structure, so she had a brief refit in July 1915 and went to the Dover Patrol and the 6th Destroyer Flotilla. In 1916 the two 4-inch breech-loaders on her fo'c'sle were replaced by a single 6-inch BL and her bridge was enlarged and strengthened. On the 20th/21st April 1917, together with *Broke*, she was in a sharp action with German destroyers making an attack on the anti-submarine barrage patrol. *Broke* rammed *G42* and *Swift* torpedoed *G85* and engaged *G42* with her 6-inch gun. Both German destroyers sank. *Swift* picked up about 100 German survivors and towed the crippled *Broke* back to Dover. She had, herself, received heavy damage in the action and, after repair and refit, rejoined the Dover Patrol in July, now with the 6-inch gun replaced by a pair of 4-inch quick-firers. She remained at Dover until the Armistice and then paid-off. She was sold for breaking up in November 1921.

Fairfield Shipbuilding & Engineering Co.Ltd., Govan, Glasgow
Launched: 11th August 1900
Displacement: 6,520 tons; (5,434 gross tons)
Length: 423 ft 6 in (pp); Beam: 51 ft 0 in; Draught: 19 ft 0 in.
Power: Two-shaft, triple expansion engines; 9,366 ihp - 19 knots.
Armament as AMC: 6 x 4.7-inch; 6 x 3-pdr.

A Royal Indian Marine troopship, taken over for service as an Armed Merchant Cruiser from August 1914 to serve on the East Indies Station throughout the war. In June 1915 she embarked French Nieuport VIs from the East Indies & Egypt Seaplane Squadron for reconnaissance purposes. In 1916 she was with the Red Sea patrol squadron and in June took part in the supporting operations for the capture of Jiddah during the Arab Revolt against Turkish rule. Also that year, she carried the 'Holy Carpet', the Kiswa, a wall hanging annually presented by Cairo for the Kaba, the Islamic shrine in Mecca. On board, accompanying the treasure from Suez to Jiddah, was an escort of 400 Egyptian troops, including artillery and cavalry. *Hardinge* carried out the same duty with the new one in 1917. In that year too, she took 400 Arab troops to El Wejh, which was captured with the help of a naval landing party. This was to deter a possible Turkish march on Mecca. In July 1917, with RIMS *Dufferin*, she took stores, 3,000 men and guns to Aqaba to supply Lawrence, who had taken the port in his land campaign and was short of food. The troops and guns were to help the defence against a possible counter-attack. She was returned to the Royal Indian Marine in May 1918.

At Port Said, 1916.

Vickers Ltd., Barrow-in-Furness
Laid down: 1907; Launched: 28th March 1908; Completed: August 1908
Displacement: 3,888 tons (2,651 gross tons)
Length: 387 ft 0 in; Beam: 46 ft 0 in; Draught: 16 ft 0 in.
Power: Three-shaft Parsons turbines; 14,500 shp - 24½ knots. 4 boilers. Coal: 552 tons
Armament: 4 x 12-pdr; 2 x 3-pdr; Added in 1916: 1 x 12-pdr HA; 1 x 2-pdr PomPom; 1 x 3-pdr field gun.
Aircraft: six seaplanes.
Complement: 172

An Isle of Man Steam Packet Co. Ship, requisitioned on 2nd January 1915 and converted to a seaplane carrier by Cammell Laird at Birkenhead. She commissioned on 23rd March 1915 and went to Harwich for a brief period and then to the Dardanelles. In August her aircraft made the first airborne torpedo attacks. On 12th, Flt. Cdr. C.H.K. Edmonds, flying Short 184 No.842, hit a 5,000 ton Turkish supply ship, dropping his torpedo from about 14ft at a range of some 300 yards. On 17th, in a second attack by Edmonds, again in No.842, his torpedo hit and set on fire the middle vessel of three steamships. On this occasion a second aircraft took part, Short 184 No.184 (the prototype), flown by Flt. Lt. G.B. Dacre. Engine trouble and the weight of the torpedo made alighting necessary, so he taxied towards the target and dropped his torpedo which hit, and sank, a tug. The now lightened aircraft took-off under rifle fire and returned to the ship. In September 1915 *Ben-My-Chree* took 300 people off the torpedoed ship *Southland* and towed her to Mudros. In January 1916 she went to Port Said to operate with the East Indies & Egypt Seaplane Squadron, and, on 14th May, the noted Naval aviator, Cdr. C.R. Samson, took command of the ship and squadron. She was briefly based at Aden in June 1916 and then returned to Port Said and the eastern Mediterranean. On 11th January 1917, while in the harbour on the French occupied island of Castellorizo, she was in an exposed position visible to the enemy on the Turkish mainland. Shots from a Turkish battery hit her and started fires in her aircraft petrol store which got out of control. She burnt out and sank. The wreck was raised and scrapped post-war.

*At Mudros c.1916. **Europa** (Diadem class cruiser of 1897) is in the background; she was the fleet flagship at Mudros from July 1915 to 1919.*

M29 – M33 Class Monitor

Workman Clark & Co.Ltd., Belfast
Laid down: March 1915; Launched: 22nd May 1915; Completed: June 1915
Displacement: 580 tons
Length: 177 ft 3 in; Beam: 31 ft 0 in; Draught: 5 ft 11 in.
Power: Two-shaft, Vertical triple expansion engines; 400 ihp – 9 knots.
2 Yarrow boilers. Oil: 45 tons. Endurance: 1,440 nm at 8 knots.
Armament: 2 x 6-inch; 1 x 6-pdr. Armour: Gunshield: 3 inch front.
Complement: 72

M32 went straight out to the Mediterranean in July 1915 and served there until December1918. She paid-off at Mudros in early 1919, returned to Britain and was then sent to the White Sea Squadron from May to September 1919. She was paid-off for disposal and sold in January 1920 for conversion to an oil tanker for the Dutch Curacao Steam Shipping Co. Renamed *Ampat*, she carried oil from the Venezuelan wells in Lake Maracaibo to the refineries on the Dutch administered island of Curacao. She had a long life, ending up, in 1946, as a French wine tanker and finally being broken up in 1951.

In Aegean waters c.1916

M15 - M28 class monitor

Sir Raylton Dixon & Co.Ltd., Middlesbrough
Laid down: March 1915; Launched: 28th June 1915; Completed: August 1915
Displacement: 570 tons
Length: 177 ft 3 in; Beam: 31 ft 0 in; Draught: 7 ft 0 in.
Power: Two-shaft, four – cylinder Bolinder oil engines (semi- diesels); 640 bhp - 10½ knots. Oil: 28 tons.
Endurance: 2,200 nm at 9½ knots.
Armament: 1 x 9.2-inch; 1 x 12-pdr; 1 x 6-pdr.
Armour: Gunshield: 4 inch front, 1¼ inch sides.
Complement: 69

Fitted out with one of the 9.2-inch guns removed from the cruiser *Grafton*, after that ship was withdrawn from the 10th Cruiser Squadron (see *Endymion*). As a new ship she, too, went into service in the Mediterranean from September 1915. In common with the other monitors on station, she took part in numerous bombardments in support of the various stages of the land campaign. However, in the early hours of the 20th January 1918 she was anchored in Kisu Bay, Imbros, together with the larger monitor *Raglan*. Both ships were caught in the surprise raid by *Goeben* and *Breslau*. *M28* was hit by *Goeben*'s second salvo and a fierce cordite fire was started. She blew up at 0627; eleven men were killed.

Off the Belgian coast in 1916

1913 Programme M Class Destroyer

R. & W. Hawthorn, Leslie & Co., Hebburn on Tyne
Laid down: 9th July 1913; Launched: 21st August 1914; Completed: January 1915
Displacement: 1,098 tons (norm.); 1,198 tons (deep load)
Length: 271 ft 6 in; Beam: 27 ft 0 in; Draught: 10 ft 6 in.
Power: Two-shaft Parsons turbines; 27,000 shp - 35 knots. 4 Yarrow boilers.
Oil: 220 tons. Endurance: 1,650 nm at 15 knots.
Armament: 3 x 4-inch; 1 x 2-pdr; 2 x 1-pdr PomPoms; 4 x 21-inch torpedo tubes.
Complement: 76

Early in 1915 she joined the 10th Destroyer Flotilla, Harwich Force. While escorting the minelayer *Princess Margaret* in the Heligoland Bight, on the night of 17/18th August 1915, she was hit by a torpedo from the German destroyer *B98*. The whole of her bow structure, underwater, was blown away, leaving the focsle deck hanging vertically down forward of the gun. In a dangerously vulnerable position, alone, close to the enemy coast, her crew made temporary repairs which allowed her to get underway. She managed to reach 10 knots and thus made the 360 mile return trip to Harwich safely. Repairs, taking a month, were carried out at Chatham. She was lent to the Dover Patrol from February 1917 to 1918. Further drama came in 1917. In the night destroyer action on 20th/21st April, when *Broke* was badly damaged, *Mentor* assisted in the towing of that ship back to Dover. Three weeks later, on 9th May, she sank *UC-26* in the Thames Estuary, with *Milne* and *Miranda*. *Mentor* was sold for breaking up in May 1921.

Off the Flanders coast in 1916

Talisman Class Destroyer

R.&W. Hawthorn, Leslie & Co., Hebburn on Tyne
Laid down: 17th December 1914; Launched: 26th August 1915; Completed: March 1916
Displacement: 1,098 tons (norm.); 1,216 tons (deep Load)
Length: 309 ft 0 in; Beam: 28 ft 7 in; Draught: 9ft 6 in.
Power: Three-shaft Parsons turbines; 25,000 shp - 32 knots. 3 Yarrow boilers.
Oil: 237 tons.
Armament: 5 x 4-inch; 4 x 21-inch torpedo tubes.
Complement: 102

She was also in the 10th Flotilla, Harwich Force, but a temporary attachment to the 13th Flotilla saw her appearance at the Battle of Jutland, where she was part of the screen for the battlegrounds. Later in 1916, and into 1917, she was with submarine flotillas and then went to the Dover Patrol until the end of the war. A bad spot in her career came on the 14th/15th February 1918. On that night, one of the numerous German destroyer forays into the Channel achieved a notable success. Seven vessels attacked the barrage minefield patrol drifters and sank eight of them, with a further seven damaged. *Termagant* was patrolling with *Amazon* and, although the German ships were sighted, they were not identified as the enemy and no action was taken. Both ships' captains were court-martialled and relieved of command. She was another of the many destroyers quickly disposed of after the war, being sold in May 1921.

S. McKnight & Co., Ayr
Launched: 17th April 1894
438 gross tons.
Length: 225 ft 0 in (pp); Beam: 26 ft 1 in; Draught: 9ft 6 in.
Power: Two-cylinder, compound diagonal engine; 277 nhp.
Armament: 1 x 12-pdr AA; 1 x 6-pdr AA.

One of the pleasure steamers belonging to P. & A Campbell of Bristol, *Westward Ho* was requisitioned and converted for minesweeping, serving from 4th November 1914 to 20th May 1919. She was with the hired paddlers based at Grimsby in 1915. On the 15th August, while sweeping near Smith's Knoll with three others, the German submarine *UB-4* was seen to be attacking some Lowestoft fishing smacks. The paddlers slipped sweeps and made for the raider, opening fire, which succeeded in driving off the U-boat. Later the same day, *UB-4* was sunk by *Inverlyon*, another Lowestoft smack, operating as a decoy vessel and armed only with a 3-pdr gun. For seemingly no good reason she was to be renamed, rather late-in-the-day, as *Westhope* in June 1918, this quickly being changed to *Western Queen*. By the end of the war she was stationed with the hired paddlers on the Tyne. After her naval service she returned to her owners to resume her normal pleasure work as *Westward Ho* for a further twenty years, until again being called to duty as an auxiliary minesweeper in the Second World War. This ship's name is often quoted as including an exclamation mark, but unlike the north Devon resort, which in turn was named after the 1855 novel by Charles Kingsley, she did not have one.

In the Edinburgh Channel in 1916

William Denny & Brothers, Dumbarton
Launched: 1890
458 gross tons.
Length: 246 ft 0 in (pp); Beam: 26 ft 6 in; Draught: 9 ft 6 in.
Power: Three-cylinder triple expansion engines; 161 nhp - 17 knots. 2 boilers
Armament: 2 x 6-pdr AA.

This pleasure steamer was from the fleet owned by the dully-named Coast Development Corporation Ltd., formerly the more pleasant-sounding Belle Steamers Ltd. Her minesweeping service was from 16th August 1915 to 8th November 1919. She was the leader of the Nore paddlers from 1915 to 1917, based first at Sheerness and then at Harwich. Early on, she picked up survivors from the paddle minesweeper *Duchess of Hamilton*, which sank after striking a mine in the Thames estuary on 29th November 1915. In 1918 she was with the Liverpool hired paddlers. She returned to civilian ownership and was broken up in 1929.

Off the East African coast in 1916

Sir James Laing & Sons, Sunderland
Launched: 1900
4,120 gross tons.
Length: 361 ft 0 in (pp); Beam: 47 ft 0 in; Draught: 26 ft 0 in.
Power: Single-shaft triple expansion engine; 12 knots.
Armament: 1 x 12-pdr; 1 x 3-pdr AA; 2 x 6-pdr AA added in 1916.
Balloon equipment: Silicol hydrogen gas generator, compressor, winch, balloon platform/well.
One Short 827 or 184 seaplane carried 1916-1917.
Kite Balloon: Spencer Type H (copy of the German Parseval Drachen type);
Envelope length: 79 ft 3 in; Diameter: 22 ft 5 in; Hydrogen Gas Capacity: c.16,000 cu.ft.

She was a cargo ship built for Bucknall Steamship Lines Ltd., but by the time of her hiring for naval service, her owners had become the Ellerman & Bucknall Steamship Co.Ltd. In March 1915 she went to H. Grayson & Co., Birkenhead for conversion to a kite balloon ship, and, after a simple transformation, she was sent out to Mudros in April. Ten days after her arrival, on 19th April, she first lofted her balloon to spot for the cruiser *Bacchante*. Her balloon also provided spotting during the Gallipoli campaign from 25th April until September. The shortcomings of her simple wooden balloon platform led to her return home for a more extensive refit. She was purchased from her owners and Cammell Laird & Co. gave her a balloon well 92 ft by 30 ft forward. When completed she was sent to Zanzibar, East Africa, in April 1916. She supported the coastal operations there until May 1917 and then returned home, being renamed *Huntball*. Her White Ensign service ended on 19th August 1917 and she subsequently worked as a Red Ensign collier numbered Y3.313 until June 1918. In 1922 she was sold to the Anglo-Saxon Petroleum Co. as *Phorus*, finally being broken up in 1931.

TB98 Class Torpedo Boat

J.I. Thornycroft & Co.Ltd., Chiswick
Launched: 1901
Displacement: 185 tons
Length: 166 ft 0 in; Beam: 17 ft 0 in; Draught: 5 ft 10 in.
Power: Single-shaft, triple expansion engine; 3,000 ihp - 25 knots.
Coal: 18 tons. Endurance: 3,150 naut. miles at 10 knots.
Armament: 3 x 3-pdr; 3 x 14-inch torpedo tubes.

This is a representative of the larger type of the old torpedo boats, many of which gave useful service in the 1914-18 conflict in the local defence flotillas based at Portsmouth and Devonport. Very little information can be found concerning their individual service but this boat is possibly in the Bristol Channel. It is included here to show the conditions which might be met with by these small craft in any wind. Her White Ensign is well out and the long swell is showing her waterline amidships while her turtle-back focsle is almost awash. Also visible are the torpedo tube positions - one just aft of the screen at the break of the focsle, which had a twin on the starboard side, and the third ahead of the barely distinguishable mainmast from which the ensign is streaming. *TB107* was eventually sold in July 1920.

*In similar conditions, but away from the coast, **Sheldrake** is digging into the swell too. This shot also shows the torpedo tubes well, only two, but for 21 in torpedoes – one ahead and one aft of the searchlight bandstand.*

Acorn class destroyer (H class from 1913)

William Denny & Brothers, Dumbarton
Laid down: 15th January 1910: Launched: 18th January 1911; Completed: May 1911
Displacement: 765 tons (norm.)
Length: 246 ft 0 in; Beam: 25 ft 4 in; Draught: 8 ft by 6 in.
Power: Three-shaft Parsons turbines; 13,500 shp - 27 knots. 4 Yarrow boilers.
Oil: 170 tons.
Armament: 2 x 4-inch; 2 x 12-pdr; 2 x 21-inch torpedo tubes.
Complement: 72

At the outbreak of war she was in the 2nd Destroyer Flotilla which became part of the Grand Fleet in August and with which it remained until the spring of 1916. The Flotilla then went to Devonport but the ships were in the process of being despatched to the Mediterranean, all surviving members being there by 1918. **Sheldrake** was on escort duty with the Western Patrol between Gibraltar and Malta, on which duty she was photographed. She was sold to breakers in May 1921.

This was a notable ship which ended her life with the Royal Navy, serving in the vital role of netlayer, the task she is shown carrying out here. These were the boom nets to protect anchorages against incursion by submarines.

Caird & Co., Greenock
Launched: 1882
1,564 gross tons
Length: 330 ft 7 in (pp); Beam: 38 ft 1 in; Draught: 15 ft 0 in.
Power: Two-cylinder compound engine; 4,500 ihp - 18 knots.
Armament: 1 x 12-pdr; 1 x 6-pdr.

She was built for the Isle of Man Steam Packet Co.Ltd. and was, at the time, the largest ship to join their fleet. She was their first steel vessel and the first to have compound oscillating machinery. This latter had a low-pressure cylinder of 112-in diameter with a stroke of 90-in, the manufacture of which was a considerable achievement in terms of the skill of the patternmakers, moulders, foundrymen and machinists involved. She was purchased for the Navy in September 1915 and served until the end of the war, being sold for breaking up in August 1919. An impressive detail to ponder is that she was still in good shape for the Navy's use in 1915, when she had already seen 33 years in service as a passenger ferry.

Fairfield Shipbuiding & Engineering Co.Ltd., Govan, Glasgow
Launched: 14th April 1887
1,657 gross tons
Length: 330 ft 5 in (pp); Beam: 39 ft 1 in; Draught: 15ft 2 in.
Power: Two-cylinder compound diagonal engine; 6,500ihp - 23 knots.
Armament: 1 x 3-pdr.

A fleet-mate of **Mona's Isle**, but five years younger, she was built as **Prince of Wales** but renamed for Naval service because of the battleship already with that name. She was of similar dimensions to her semi-sister and also had a 112-inch diameter low-pressure cylinder but fixed, not oscillating. An increase of 2,000 horsepower also gave her more speed. Purchased on 28th January 1915 for the Navy, she is also shown laying her nets; two of the floats are visible in her wake in this photograph, understood to have been taken in the Aegean. She was sold for breaking up in February 1920.

As she appeared in 1916

Sir W.G. Armstrong, Whitworth & Co.Ltd., Elswick
Laid down: 14th September 1911; Launched: 22nd January 1913; Completed: August 1914
Displacement: 27,850 tons (norm.); 31,620 tons (full load, by 1918)
Length: 671 ft 6 in; Beam: 89 ft 0 in; Draught: 28 ft 1 in (deep)
Power: Four-shaft Parsons turbines; 34,000 shp - 22 knots.
22 Babcock & Wilcox boilers. Coal: 1,500 tons (norm.), 3,200 tons (max.)
Oil: 620 tons. Endurance: c.4,500 nm at 10 knots.
Armament: 14 x 12-inch; 20 x 6-inch; 10 x 3-inch; 4 x 3-pdr; 3 x 21-inch torpedo tubes;
later, 2 x 3-inch AA added.
Armour: Belt: 9 - 4 inch; Deck 2½ - 1 inch; Turret 12 - 8 inch; Barbette 9 - 2 inch; Conning tower 12 - 4 inch.
Complement: 1,115 in 1914; 1,267 by 1918.

Like *Erin*, she was being built for the Turkish Navy and was seized on 2nd August 1914, two days before the outbreak of war. She was originally ordered by Brazil, with the intended name *Rio de Janeiro*, but financial problems in that country led to her being sold to Turkey in January 1914 and renamed *Sultan Osman I*. On being taken over for the Royal Navy she underwent alterations, principally the removal of a flying boat-deck over the turrets between the funnels, and of her torpedo nets. She was soon ready to join the 4th Battle Squadron, Grand Fleet on the 28th August 1914. In 1915 she went to the 1st Battle Squadron. In 1916 her tripod mainmast was removed and replaced by a pole mast as shown in the photograph. She was at the Battle of Jutland. (*service career notes continue on page 108*)

Blyth Shipbuilding & Drydock Co.Ltd., Blyth
Laid down: 7th November 1913; Launched: 5th September 1914; Completed: December 1914
Displacement: 7,080 tons (norm.); 7,450 tons (load)
Length: 366 ft 0 in; Beam: 50 ft 10 in; Draught: 18ft 0 in.
Power: Single-shaft triple expansion engine; 3,000 ihp - 11 knots.
2 boilers. Oil: 500 tons.
Armament: 4 x 12-pdr; Aircraft: Various - e.g: 4 to 6 seaplanes or 5 seaplanes and 2 landplanes.
Hangar - 150 ft by 54 ft; sliding hatch 40 ft by 30 ft; 2 x 3 ton steam cranes for handling aircraft.
Complement: 180

A cargo ship, in the early stages of building, was purchased in May 1914 by the Admiralty for completion to new plans for a purpose-designed aircraft carrier. After commissioning and trials she left for the Dardanelles in February 1915, arriving at Tenedos on the 17th. With six seaplanes onboard, she carried out aerial reconnaissance for the bombardment of Turkish Forts and covered the Gallipoli landings from 25th April. At the end of May she went to Imbros where her principal role became that of a depot ship for No.2 Wing, Royal Naval Air Service, which role occupied most of her time until the end of the war. Postwar she was on various duties in the Black Sea, off Somaliland and in the Persian Gulf, until returning home for a refit in November 1920. After a period in reserve, in September 1922 she ferried aircraft out East during the Turkish Chanak Crisis; in 1923 she became a depot ship and in 1934 relinquished her name for the new aircraft carrier, and was renamed *Pegasus*. She was next a catapult trials ship and in 1941 was operating as a catapult ship for convoy escort. When escort carriers began to appear she reverted to the depot ship role. Sold in 1946 for a proposed conversion to a merchant ship which did not materialize, she was again sold to breakers in 1949.

Inside the hangar during the period in 1916 when she was parent ship for No.2 Wing. The aircraft in the centre is an example of the later version of the Sopwith Schneider, with ailerons instead of wing-warping. Between April 1916 and March 1918 at least ten of this type passed through her hands for repair and maintenance.

At Mudros in 1916

TB13-36 Class Torpedo Boat

William Denny & Brothers, Dumbarton
Laid down: 20th February 1908; Launched: 29th September 1908; Completed: January 1910

(For class data notes, see *TB15* page 35)

This example of the final group of torpedo boats, known as 'oily wads', shows some of the alterations made for their wartime service. The openings under the bridge are screened in with canvas, on which her number has been painted, in addition to being carried on her aft funnel. She has a pole mainmast and a pair of carley floats abreast the funnels. The torpedo boats' duties in the Mediterranean would have been much the same as they were for those in home waters, that is anti-submarine escort and patrolling . She was sold for breaking up at Malta in November 1919. In the background is *Blenheim* (Blake class cruiser of 1890) which was converted to a depot ship in 1907-8. She was sent to Mudros in March 1915 to act as depot ship for the Mediterranean destroyer flotillas operating in the Aegean.

Acorn Class Destroyer

J. Samuel White & Co.Ltd., Cowes
Laid down: 10th December 1909; Launched: 24th June 1910; Completed: February 1911
(For class data notes, see *Sheldrake* page 65 - except: 4 White-Forster boilers)

She was sister of *Sheldrake* and her service followed the same pattern as noted for that ship except that her area of operations was in the Eastern Mediterranean and Aegean waters. She is shown here passing through the boom at Mudros and, as seems to have been the case in this area of operations, does not have her pennant number painted on her hull. She was sold for breaking up in May 1921.

*In Scapa Flow in 1916. On the right, almost invisible against the background is **St. Vincent***

Orion Class Battleship

William Beardmore & Co.Ltd., Dalmuir
Laid down: 5th April 1910; Launched: 1st May 1911; Completed: November 1912
Displacement: 21,900 tons (norm.) 28,430 tons (deep load, in 1918)
Length 581 ft 0 in; Beam: 88 ft 6 in; Draught: 28 ft 9 in, 31 ft 3 in (deep)
Power: Four-shaft Parsons turbines; 27,000 shp - 21 knots. 18 Yarrow boilers.
Coal: 900 tons, 3,300 tons (max.); Oil: 800 tons. Endurance: 6,730 nm at 10 knots on coal plus oil.
Armament: 10 x 13.5-inch; 16 x 4-inch; 4 x 3-pdr; 3 x 21-inch torpedo tubes;
later - 13 x 4-inch; 1 x 4-inch AA
Armour: Belt: 12 - 4 inch; Deck: 4 - 1 inch; Turret: 11 inch; Barbette: 10 - 2 inch; Conning tower: 11 inch.
Complement: c.750, c.1,100 by 1917

Although this class had all five turrets on the centre-line, the foremast was positioned behind the fore-funnel, as in **Dreadnought**, a feature which had already been shown to produce intolerable conditions in the control top with the rising heat, smoke and gasses from the funnel. The Orions were the last ships with this layout. At the outbreak of war, **Conqueror** was in the 2nd Battle Squadron, which then became part of the Grand Fleet. On 27th December, she was in a collision with her sister, **Monarch**, which left her with bows severely damaged. Initial repairs were carried out at Scapa, then she was taken to Invergordon and Devonport. She did not rejoin the fleet until March 1915. She was at the Battle of Jutland; after which, in common with the other battleships, she carried out the various sweeps and patrols which occupied the next two-and-a –half years. Postwar she was with the 3rd Battle Squadron from March to October 1919. The Washington Treaty obligations led to her sale to breakers in December 1922.

In the Mediterranean in 1916

Halcyon or Dryad Class Torpedo Gunboat

H.M. Dockyard, Devonport
Laid down: 21st January 1893; Launched: 20th February 1894; Completed: February 1895
Displacement: 1,105 tons (norm.), 1,210 (full load)
Length: 262 ft 6 in; Beam: 30 ft 6 in; Draught: 11 ft 6 in.
Power: Two-shaft triple expansion engines; 3,500 ihp (forced draught) - 18 knots.
2 boilers. Coal: 100/200 tons. Endurance: 1,850 naut.miles at 10 knots.
Armament: 2 x 4.7-inch; 4 x 6-pdr; 5 x 18-inch torpedo tubes (2 reloads carried).
Complement: 120

From 1906 to 1914 she served as a tender to the Navigation School at Portsmouth then, when war came, she was converted to a minesweeper. In 1915 she was in the Downs Boarding Flotilla and then was sent out to the Mediterranean. Nothing of note seems to be recorded of her career there but she was probably mostly employed on escorting duties. She was sold for breaking up in February 1920.

Arabis Class (Flower Class) Fleet Sweeping Sloop

Ropner & Sons Ltd., Stockton on Tees
Launched: 21st December 1915
Displacement: 1,250 tons.
Length: 268 ft 0 in; Beam: 33 ft 6 in; Draught:11 ft 0 in.
Power: Single-shaft triple expansion engine; 2,000 ihp - 16 knots. 2 boilers.
Coal: 130/250 tons. Endurance: 2,200 nm at 15 knots.
Armament: 2 x 4.7-inch; 2 x 3-pdr AA.
Complement: 90

Delivered to the Navy in February 1916, she was sent to join the Western Patrol in the Straits of Gibraltar, and escorting convoys between Gibraltar and Malta, as shown here. Later she operated further east and, towards the end of the war, on 4th October 1918, she, together with the trawler *Cradosin*, damaged *UB-68* in the Ionian Sea. Damage was such that the submarine was scuttled by her crew. *Snapdragon* continued in service after the war until being sold in May 1934.

Insect Class River Gunboat

Barclay Curle & Co.Ltd., Whiteinch, Glasgow
Launched: 16th December 1915
Displacement: 645 tons.
Length: 237 ft 6 in; Beam: 36 ft 0 in; Draught: 4 ft 0 in.
Power: Two-shaft triple expansion engines; 2000 ihp – 14 knots; (propellers in tunnels). 2 Yarrow boilers.
Coal: 35 tons; Oil: 54 tons.
Armament: 2 x 6-inch; 2 x 12-pdr; 6 x 0.303 Maxim machine guns.
Complement: 53

These ships were ordered under the cover description of 'Large China Gunboats' to disguise the actual planned purpose of operating on the River Danube against the Austro-Hungarian River Flotilla. This was not put into effect due to the changing military situation in the area, and they therefore served in other theatres, acting as small monitors to support the land operations. In 1916, *Cockchafer* was one of four of the class temporarily rearmed with 6-inch QF MKII guns on CPII anti-aircraft mountings with 53½ degrees elevation, for use against Zeppelins. They were positioned on the east coast, *Cockchafer* being sent to Brightlingsea, where she is shown in the photograph, with the high-angle gun forward of the bridge. In September 1918 she went to North Russia for operations on the Dvina River. After the war, many of the class did go to the China Station, *Cockchafer* being towed out to Hong Kong in 1920. She was eventually sold in 1949 at Singapore.

Improved Marksman Class/Parker Class, Flotilla Leader

Cammell Laird & Co.Ltd., Birkenhead
Laid down: c.November 1915; Launched: 16th August 1916; Completed: November 1916
Displacement: 1,666 tons (norm.), c.1,900 tons (deep load)
Length: 325 ft 0 in; Beam: 31 ft 9 in; Draught: 12 ft 0 in.
Power: Three-shaft Parsons turbines; 36,000 shp - 34 knots. 4 Yarrow boilers. Oil: 515 tons.
Armament: 4 x 4-inch; 2 x 2-pdr PomPoms; 4 x 21-inch torpedo tubes.
Complement: 116

Having joined the Grand Fleet as leader of the 13th Destroyer Flotilla in November 1916, *Hoste* was to have a very short career. On 19th December, the Grand Fleet was on exercises in bad weather. Next day, *Hoste*'s helm jammed at 25 knots. She managed to escape collision with her consorts and stopped to make temporary repairs. She got under way again and made for Scapa, escorted by *Negro*. The weather worsened, and in the south-easterly gale her steering failed again, causing her to turn abruptly to starboard across *Negro*'s bows. With no time to react, *Negro* struck *Hoste*'s stern, knocking two depth charges off which exploded at their set depth. The blast shattered *Hoste*'s stern and blew in the bottom of *Negro* under the engine room. The latter's damaged hull failed under the strain of the weather and she quickly sank. *Hoste* managed to get slowly underway again but three hours later her back broke, leaving the stern supported by the propeller-shafts and the engine room flooding. In a magnificent display of seamanship, in appalling weather, *Marvel* came alongside the focsle 13 times, receiving severe damage herself, but rescuing *Hoste*'s entire crew but for four. *Hoste*'s shattered remains sank five minutes later.

Ascot/Racecourse Class Paddle Minesweeper

A.McMillan & Sons Ltd., Dumbarton
Launched: 17th May 1916
Displacement: 810 tons.
Length: 245 ft 9 in; Beam: 29 ft 0 in, 58 ft 0 in over paddle-boxes; Draught: 7 ft 0 in.
Power: Two-cylinder diagonal compound engines; 1,500 ihp - 14½ knots. Coal: 156 tons.
Armament: 1 x 12-pdr; 1 x 3-inch AA; Four depth charges plus lance bombs.
Complement: 50

The design for this class was based on Ailsa Shipbuilding's **Glen Usk** which had been taken up for service as a minesweeper in 1915. In July 1916, **Totnes** was sent to the east coast to become the leader for the Lowestoft paddlers. On 29th December, paired with **Ludlow** and with further sisters in company, she was sweeping off the Shipwash Lightship. Both **Totnes** and **Ludlow** were mined within a few minutes of each other. **Totnes** had her bow blown off but was taken in tow by her sister **Cheltenham**, which brought her back to Harwich where tugs came out to bring her into the harbour. **Ludlow**, which had lost her stern, sank during the night. After being repaired, **Totnes** was made the leader of the Stornoway paddlers in 1917, and in 1918 she was leader of the Oban Fleet Sweeping Flotilla. Postwar, she led the 16th FSF and was sold in March 1922.

Robust Class Paddle Tug

H.M. Dockyard, Chatham
Launched: 4th September 1908
Displacement: 690 tons.
Length: 152 ft 6 in; Beam: 27 ft 3 in, 50 ft 6 in over paddle-boxes; Draught: 11 ft 0 in.
Power: Two-cylinder diagonal compound engines; 1,250 ihp - 12 knots. 2 boilers.
Coal: 103 tons.
Complement: 17

As a Portsmouth harbour tug, she serves as a representative for the multitude of these vessels, both naval and requisitioned, paddle and screw, which operated at the many ports and anchorages used by the Royal Navy in the British Isles and at overseas bases. After a long career, she was finally disposed of at Dover breakers in May 1957.

Astraea Class Cruiser

H.M. Dockyard, Devonport
Launched: 2nd December 1892; Completed: July 1894
Displacement: 4,360 tons.
Length: 339 ft 6 in; Beam: 49 ft 6 in; Draught: 19 ft 0 in.
Power: Two-shaft, three-cylinder triple expansion engines; 9,500 ihp (forced draught) - 19½ knots.
8 cylindrical boilers. Coal: 1,000 tons.
Armament: 2 x 6-inch; 8 x 4.7-inch; 10 x 6-pdr; 3 x 18-inch torpedo tubes.
As Depot Ship: 2 x 6-inch; 2 x 6-pdr; 4 x 3-pdr; (4 x 3-pdr only, in 1917).
Armour: Deck: 2 inch; six-inch gunshield: 4½ inch; conning tower: 3 inch
Complement: 318 (as Cruiser)

In May 1906 she paid-off at Devonport, having returned home from the Pacific Squadron. She was sent to Haulbowline Dockyard, Cork, for conversion to a submarine depot ship and completed in April 1907. In the war she was the depot ship for the 6th Submarine Flotilla from 1914 – 1916, and the 2nd Submarine Flotilla, 1916 – 1918. The location of this photo is uncertain but might be Gibraltar although, as the above noted flotillas were home-based throughout the war, it is not clear what she was doing there. She was sold for breaking up in April 1920.

Fairfield Shipbuilding & Engineering Co.Ltd., Govan, Glasgow
Laid down: 25th January 1915; Launched: 4th March 1916; Completed: September 1916
Displacement: 27,947 tons (load) 32,727 tons (deep load)
Length: 794 ft 0 in; Beam: 90 ft 0 in; Draught: 27 ft 0 in (load), 30 ft 0 in (deep load)
Power: Four-shaft, Brown-Curtis turbines; 112,000 shp - 31½ knots.
42 Babcock & Wilcox boilers. Oil: 1,000 tons (min.), 4,289 tons (max.).
Endurance: 4,700 nm at 12 knots.
Armament: 6 x 15-inch; 17 x 4-inch; 2 x 3-inch AA; 4 x 3-pdr; 10 x 21-inch torpedo tubes.
Armour: Belt: 6 - 1½ inch; Deck: 2 - ¾ inch; Turret: 11 - 7 inch; Barbette: 7 - 4 inch;
Conning tower: 10 - 6 inch.
Complement: 953 in 1916, c.1,100 in 1918

She joined the 1st Battlecruiser Squadron, Grand Fleet, in September 1916 but did not become operational until early 1917 and saw no significant action during the war. Postwar she was with the Atlantic Fleet BCS. She was refitted to take HRH the Prince of Wales on the Royal Tour to Australia and New Zealand in 1920-21 and to India and Japan 1921-22. In refit from 1923-26 and then extensively reconstructed between 1936 and 1939. She served throughout the Second World War, being the last British battlecruiser in service after the losses of *Hood*, and her sister, *Repulse*, and was sold for breaking up in 1948.

Active Class Cruiser

H.M. Dockyard, Pembroke
Laid down: 27th July 1910; Launched: 14th March 1911; Completed: December 1911
Displacement: 3,440 tons (norm.); 4,000 tons (deep load)
Length: 406 ft 0 in; Beam: 41 ft 6 in; Draught: 14 ft 0 in (norm.), 15 ft 7 in (deep).
Power: Four-shaft Parsons turbines; 18,000 shp - 25 knots. 12 Yarrow boilers.
Coal: 780 tons. Oil: 190 tons.
Armament: 10 x 4-inch; 4 x 3-pdr; 2 x 18-inch torpedo tubes.
Armour: Deck: 1 inch; Conning tower: 4 inch.
Complement: 320

At the outbreak of war she was the leader of the 2nd Destroyer Flotilla and joined the Harwich Force; in 1915, transferred to the Grand Fleet, then, in 1916-17, she led the 4th Destroyer Flotilla at Portsmouth with attachments to the Dover Patrol. This photograph is from 1917, when she had been fitted with a 3-inch AA gun on a bandstand aft. She is shown while escorting a paddle minesweeper flotilla. In 1917-18 she was based at Queenstown and spent the last months of the war in the Mediterranean. She was sold for breaking up in April 1920.

Workman Clark & Co.Ltd., Belfast
Launched: 25th August 1904
10,635 gross tons.
Length: 540 ft 0 in; Beam: 60 ft 6 in; Draught: 38 ft 0 in.
Power: Three-shaft, steam turbines; 10,000 shp - 17½ knots.
Armament: 8 x 4.7-inch, originally; from March 1915 - 6 x 6-inch; 2 x 6-pdr.

This liner belonged to the Allan Line of Glasgow. As an Armed Merchant Cruiser, her period of service was 17th August 1914 to 31st January 1920. Initially based at Gibraltar with the 9th Cruiser Squadron for patrol duties in the Canary Islands area and off the west coast of Africa; in March 1915, she was re-equipped with 6-inch guns to join the 10th Cruiser Squadron on the Northern Patrol, after withdrawal of the old cruisers. From mid 1917 she was on convoy escort duties. She was returned to her owners in 1920 and went to the breakers in 1929.

J Class Submarine

H.M. Dockyard, Devonport
Launched: 9th September 1915
Displacement: 1,204 tons (surface), 1,820 tons (submerged)
Length: 275 ft 6 in; Beam: 23 ft 0 in; Draught: 14 ft 0 in.
Power: Three-shaft, 12 cylinder Vickers diesels; 3,600hp/electric motors;
1,350 hp – 19½ knots (surface), 9½ knots (submerged). Fuel: 80 tons.
Range: 5,000 naut. miles at 12½ knots on surface.
Armament: 1 x 12-pdr AA (replaced by 1 x 4-inch); 6 x 18-inch torpedo tubes, 12 torpedoes carried.
Complement: 44

From completion until the end of the war, she was with the 11th Submarine Flotilla based at Blyth, on patrols in the North Sea. She was presented to the Royal Australian Navy in March 1919, together with the other five surviving members of the class; broken up in Melbourne in 1924.

In 1917 when A and Y turret roofs were painted dark grey, the colour being carried over onto the upper part of the sides. This was in preparation for the application of deflection scales in white, which appears not yet to have been carried out.

Sir W.G.Armstrong, Whitworth & Co.Ltd., Elswick
Laid down: December 1911; Launched: 27th November 1913; Completed: September 1915
Displacement: 28,622 tons (norm.), 32,188 tons (deep load)
Length: 661 ft 0 in; Beam: 92 ft 0 in; Draught: 29 ft 6 in (norm.), 31 ft 11 in (deep)
Power: Four-shaft, Brown-Curtis (high pressure)/Parsons (low pressure) turbines; 37,000 shp - 22½ knots.
21 Yarrow type boilers by John Brown.
Coal: 1,050/3,300 tons. Oil: 520 tons. Endurance: 4,400 nm at 10 knots.
Armament: 10 x 14-inch; 18 x 6-inch (reduced by two in 1917); 2 x 3-inch AA; 4 x 21-inch torpedo tubes.
Armour: Belt 9 - 4 inch; Deck 4 - 1 inch; Turret 10 - 3 inch; Barbette 10 - 4 inch;
Conning tower 11 -3 inch.
Complement: c.1,170

She was laid down for Chile as ***Almirante Latorre*** (originally to have been ***Valparaiso***) and was being fitted-out when war broke out. Construction was suspended until the ship was purchased for the Royal Navy on 9th September 1914 and fitting-out restarted. In October 1915 she joined the 4th Battle Squadron, Grand Fleet. She was at Jutland and then went to the 1st Battle Squadron. After being placed in reserve in March 1919, she was refitted at Devonport and returned to Chile, as ***Almirante Latorre***, in November 1920. She served in the Chilean Navy until 1959 when she was sold to breakers in Japan.

*In June 1917 with the Japanese destroyer **Sakaki** alongside after having her damaged forepart cut off with oxy-acetylene burners.*

Launched: 1889
741 gross tons
Length:90 ft 0 in; Beam: 20ft 0 in.

This was the tug/salvage vessel **Dalhousie**, purchased in March 1916, and renamed. She operated in the Mediterranean. On 11th April 1918 the merchant ship **Kingstonian** was damaged in a submarine attack and was taken to the anchorage in Carloforte Bay, San Pietro Island, Sardinia. **Dalkeith** was sent to attend to her, arriving on the 28th and securing alongside with the rescue tug **Moose** outboard of her. At 0540 on the 29th April, a torpedo fired by **UB-48** passed under the tug and **Dalkeith** and exploded under **Kingstonian**'s boiler room. This also blew a hole in **Dalkeith**'s hull and she rapidly flooded and sank within two minutes. The submarine surfaced and opened fire with her gun, hitting **Moose**, and then escaped. Nine of **Dalkeith**'s men were lost, including hired Greek crew members.

Sakaki was one of five of her class to serve in the Mediterranean in 1917-18. She had been torpedoed by the Austrian **U-27** on 11th June 1917. The hull was cut just aft of the position of the forefunnel, about a third of the ship's length being lost. She was repaired-rebuilt and returned to Japan, with her sisters, in December 1919. Japan had been asked, in January 1917, to send destroyers to the Mediterranean to relieve the overstretched anti-submarine forces. A cruiser and eight destroyers, including the above five, arrived in Malta in April. Later in the year, one cruiser and a further four destroyers were sent.

Marksman/Lightfoot Class Flotilla Leader

R. &W. Hawthorn, Leslie & Co., Hebburn on Tyne
Laid down: 20th July 1914; Launched: 28th April 1915; Completed: November 1915
Displacement: 1,607 tons (norm.), 1,865 tons (deep load)
Length: 324 ft 10 in; Beam: 31 ft 9 in; Draught: 12 ft 0 in.
Power: Three-shaft Brown-Curtis turbines; 36,000 shp - 34 knots; 4 Yarrow boilers.
Oil:413/515 tons. Endurance: 4,290 nm at 15 knots.
Armament: 4 x 4-inch; 2 x 2-pdr; 4 x 21-inch torpedo tubes. In July 1918, *Marksman* received two sets of
depth charge racks for 25 depth charges, plus two depth charge throwers.
Complement: 104

She joined the Grand Fleet and was leader for the M class destroyers of the 12th Destroyer Flotilla. She was at Jutland, where, on 1st June, she picked up survivors from British destroyers sunk in the night action. Remaining with the Grand Fleet into 1917, in August that year she transferred to Dover and the 6th Destroyer Flotilla until March 1918. She then went back north to be based at Dundee for the Northern Patrol. While escorting a convoy on 1st November, she collided with the trawler, ***Charles Hammond***, off Kirkaldy in a gale. She sent a party of men onboard to assist in trying to save the ship, but the trawler sank next day. *Marksman* was sold to the breakers in November 1921.

Launched: 1906
84 gross tons
Armament: 1 x 6-pdr AA

This Inverness drifter is typical of the many of these small fishing vessels which were taken into service. She was hired in August 1915 and equipped with anti-submarine nets, which were nets with mines attached, in which it was hoped U-boats would be caught and destroyed. She returned to her owners in 1919.

In 1917, after her bridge was enlarged and extended and her aft control position, on the dwarf tripod, converted to a searchlight platform.

H.M. Dockyard, Portsmouth
Laid down: 2nd October 1905; Launched: 10th February 1906; Completed: December 1906
Displacement: 18,120 tons (norm.), 20,730 tons (deep load)
Length: 527 ft 0 in; Beam: 82 ft 0 in; Draught: 26 ft 6 in.
Power: Four-shaft Parsons turbines; 23,000 shp - 21 knots. 18 Babcock and Wilcox boilers. Coal: 900 tons (min.), 2,900 tons (max.) Oil: 1,120 tons. Endurance: 6,620 nm at 10 knots.
Armament: 10 x 12-inch; 28 x 12-pdr; (10 x 12-pdr by 1916); 5 x 18-inch torpedo tubes.
Armour: Belt 11 - 4 inch; Deck 4 - ¾ inch; Turret/Barbette/Conning tower: 11 inch.
Complement: c.700; 810 in 1916

She was flagship of the 4th Battle Squadron, Home Fleet, in August 1914, and went to Scapa Flow on the formation of the Grand Fleet. On 18th March 1915, when returning from fleet exercises, she sighted, chased and rammed a U-boat, which sank with all hands. This was *U-29* whose commander, K.Lt. Otto Weddigen had, on 22nd September 1914 in *U-9*, sunk the armoured cruisers *Hogue*, *Cressy* and *Aboukir*. *Dreadnought* was the only battleship to sink a submarine. She had a major refit at Portsmouth in early 1916 and in May, became the flagship of the 3rd Battle Squadron of King Edward VII class pre-Dreadnoughts, at Sheerness. In March 1918 she returned to the Grand Fleet as flagship of the 4th Battle Squadron. In July she paid-off into reserve at Devonport and in February 1919, at Rosyth. Put on the sale list in March 1920, she went for breaking up in May 1921.

K Class Submarine

H.M. Dockyard, Portsmouth
Launched: 16th December 1916
Displacement: 1,980 tons (surface), 2,566 tons (submerged)
Length: 330 ft 0 in; Beam: 26 ft 6 in; Draught: 17 ft 0 in.
Power: Two-shaft Brown-Curtis geared turbines; 10,500 shp – 24 knots; 800 hp diesel engine;
4 electric motors; 1440 hp - 9½ knots (submerged); Two Yarrow Boilers.
Fuel: 170 tons. Endurance: 3,000 naut.miles at 13½ knots on surface.
Armament: 2 x 4-inch; 1 x 3-inch AA; 8 x 18-inch torpedo tubes, 18 torpedoes carried.
Complement: 59

The K class submarines were a remarkable technical achievement which was overshadowed by operational problems in connection with their planned purpose and serious accidental losses. It was hoped that they would operate with the Grand Fleet using their fast surface speed and ability to act as submersible destroyers. A major factor in preventing their success in this role was the time it took to submerge. When running on the surface the turbines had to be stopped and cooled, funnels retracted and capped, diesel started to attain diving speed and then transferring to the batteries for running submerged. This aerial photo shows *K5* in original condition getting up steam on her boilers. She survived her time with the Grand Fleet but was lost by an unknown cause in the Bay of Biscay in January 1921.

In Devonport Dockyard in 1917. The photograph was taken from a hospital ship, hence the ambulance train and line of motor ambulances awaiting the disembarkation of her patients.

Canopus Class Battleship

Vickers Ltd., Barrow-in-Furness
Laid down: 23rd August 1898; Launched: 25th July 1899; Completed: April 1902
(For class data notes, see ***Ocean*** page 16)

In 1913-14 she was gunnery training ship at the Nore and, on the outbreak of war, joined the 8th Battle Squadron in the Channel and on Atlantic patrols. In November 1914 she went out to West Africa for operations against the Cameroons and then to Egypt and back again to the west coast and Cape Verde. At Gibraltar in January 1915 she became flagship of Admiral Sir John de Robeck for the Dardanelles campaign. She was at the start of the attack on 19th February, bombarding Sedd-el-Bahr and Kum Kale. She covered the Cape Helles landings on 25th April. In November she returned to Egypt and subsequently served in the East Indies, Egypt again, East Africa and the Cape of Good Hope, finally returning home in 1917. The photograph dates from this period when she was being rearmed; four 6-inch, main deck, casemate guns were removed and replaced by four 6-inch, in open shields on the battery deck. On completion of the refit she became an ordnance depot at Devonport until finally paying-off in 1919. She was sold for breaking up in December 1921.

(For details of MLs see page 26)

This photograph is included to show the lively performance of the motor launches even in quite moderate conditions. No details are recorded of the boat or her career but, as she has an awning spread, it might be assumed that the location is somewhere in the Mediterranean.

Admiralty M Class Destroyer

J.I. Thornycroft & Co.Ltd., Woolston
Laid down: 20th November 1914; Launched: 12 July 1915; Completed: October 1915
Displacement: 985 tons
Length: 274 ft 0 in; Beam: 26ft 9 in; Draught: c.9 ft 0 in.
Power: Three-shaft Parsons turbines; 26,500 shp - 35 knots. 3 Yarrow boilers. Oil: 254 tons.
Armament: 3 x 4-inch; 1 x 2-pdr; 4 x 21-inch torpedo tubes.
Complement: 80

One of the numerous Grand Fleet destroyers whose valuable, but routine, service has left little in the records. However, on 20th July 1918 in the Irish Sea she, together with her sisters *Marne* and *Pidgeon*, and patrol craft, sank *UB-124*. *Milbrook* went to the breakers in September 1921.

Caledon Shipbuilding & Engineering Co., Dundee
Launched: 1910
Displacement: 3,500 tons; 1,726 gross tons
Armament: 1 x 4 -inch; 3 x 12-pdr.

A passenger-cargo vessel plying the route between London and Leith of the London & Edinburgh Shipping Co., she was hired for service as an Armed Boarding Steamer from 28th October 1914. These smaller ships operated in a similar role to the Armed Merchant Cruisers; to stop, search and detain, if necessary, foreign merchant ships which might be carrying cargo for the enemy. Owing to their size their area of operations would have been the North Sea, the Channel or Western Approaches, or in the Mediterranean. Having carried out these duties throughout the war, *Royal Scot* ran as a troop carrier from January to April 1919. She was returned to her owners on 27th December 1919; renamed *Royal Highlander* in 1930, she was sold two years later to the Columbian Navy as a transport, and named *Mosquera*. She was scrapped in 1945.

P Class Patrol Boat

Joseph T. Eltringham & Co., South Shields
Launched: 21st December 1915
Displacement: 613 tons.
Length: 244 ft 6 in; Beam; 23 ft 9 in; Draught: 8 ft 0 in.
Power: Two-shaft turbine; 3,500 shp - 20 knots. 2 boilers.
Armament: 1 x 4-inch; 1 x 2-pdr AA; 2 x 14-inch torpedo tubes.
Complement: c.50

One of the most unusual warship designs to appear during the war was that for the P boats. They were patrol boats/ utility destroyers with a low profile, intended to allow them to get close to the enemy before firing gun or torpedo or, if a submarine, to ram it. It is believed that *P27* was with the Portsmouth Escort Force; others were with the Dover Patrol and the Nore Local Defence Flotilla. She was sold for breaking up in July 1923.

*Note the white-painted chequerboard pattern on the upper part of the bridge, tripod mast and control top. The intention was to make these features less conspicuous when positioned off the enemy coast for a bombardment from behind a smokescreen laid by MLs. Her sister, **Erebus**, had a similar application but in a diamond pattern.*

Erebus Class Monitor

Harland & Wolff, Belfast
Laid down: 26th October 1915; Launched: 18th May 1916; Completed: August 1916
Displacement: 8,450 tons (deep load)
Length: 405 ft 0 in; Beam: Main hull 62 ft 0 in; over bulges 88 ft 2 in; Draught: 11 ft 8 in.
Power: Two-shaft, Four-cylinder vertical triple expansion engines; 6,000 ihp - 12 knots.
4 Babcock & Wilcox boilers. Oil: 784 tons. Endurance: 2,480 nm at 12 knots.
Armament: 2 x 15-inch; 2 x 6-inch; (later 4 x 4-inch); 2 x 3-inch HA; 1 x 3-inch AA.
Armour: Belt: 4 inch; Deck: 4 inch; Turret face: 13 inch
Complement: 204

When completed she went to the Dover Patrol in August 1916 and took part in the continuing series of bombardments of targets on the Belgian coast. In her second year of these duties, on the night of 18th/19th October 1917, she was hit by three torpedoes from German torpedo boats while lying at anchor off Dunkirk. She beached herself with considerable damage to her bows; after ensuring that she was in a safe condition, she was towed back to Dover. Setting off again for repairs at Portsmouth, she was abandoned off Hastings on the night of 27th October but was reboarded and brought into Spithead next day. The necessary repairs took 10 weeks to complete. In January 1919 she became the Director and Fire Control Training Ship at Portsmouth and was involved in trials against the old battleship *Swiftsure* and various surrendered German vessels, including submarines and the modern battleship *Baden*. These tasks were carried out in 1919-22. From 1924, still at Portsmouth, she was a turret drillship. She was refitted for service in the Second World War but was sunk off Derna on 24th February 1941. This was only after she had been damaged by Italian aircraft, mines and finally Luftwaffe Junkers Ju-88 bombers and had to be scuttled owing to her vulnerable position.

Admiralty R Class Destroyer

William Denny & Brothers, Dumbarton
Laid down: 15th October 1915; Launched: 29th August 1916; Completed: December 1916
Displacement: 1,070 tons (norm.), 1,173 tons (deep load)
Length: 276 ft 0 in; Beam: 26 ft 8 in; Draught: 9 ft 0 in.
Power: Two-shaft Brown-Curtis turbines; 27,000 shp - 36 knots. 3 Yarrow boilers. Oil: 290 tons.
Endurance: c.3,000 nm at 15 knots.
Armament: 3 x 4-inch; 1 x 2-pdr; 4 x 21-inch torpedo tubes.
Complement: 82

This is a representative of the new class which was a refinement of the preceding M class, the principal differences being two propellers instead of three and the aft 4-inch gun mounting raised on a bandstand to keep it clear of any seas sweeping along the after deck in rough weather. As with many destroyers, especially those which were completed post-Jutland, she left no particular record to history. However, she continued to serve post-war until being sold in July 1926.

*In about August 1917, with a clinker screen on the forefunnel and anti-aircraft guns aft, one on the searchlight plat-form and the other on the roof of Y turret. Visible over her focsle are the masts and funnel tops of **Collingwood**.*

Bellerophon class battleship

H.M. Dockyard, Portsmouth
Laid down: 3rd December 1906; Launched: 27th July 1907; Completed: February 1909
Displacement: 18,596 tons (norm), 22,540 tons (deep load)
Length: 526 ft 0 in; Beam: 82 ft 6 in; Draught: 27 ft 6 in (norm), 31 ft 4 in (deep).
Power: Four-shaft Parsons turbines; 23,000 shp - 21 knots. 18 Babcock and Wilcox boilers.
Coal: 900/2,648 tons. Oil: 842 tons. Endurance: 5,720 nm at 10 knots on coal & oil.
Armament: 10 x 12-inch; 16 x 4-inch; 4 x 3-pdr; 3 x 18-inch torpedo tubes.
Armour: Belt: 10 - 5 inch; Deck: 4 - ¾ inch; Barbette: 10 - 5 inch; Turret and conning tower: 11 inch.
Complement: 720, 845 by 1917

Throughout the war, from August 1914, she was in the 4th Battle Squadron, Grand Fleet and was present at Jutland. In Scapa Flow, on 9th July 1917, when the battleship *Vanguard* was destroyed by an accidental explosion, *Bellerophon* was at anchor nearby and was hit by falling debris. In March 1919 she became a turret drill-ship at the Nore (Sheerness), and in September went into reserve at Devonport. She was put up for disposal in 1920 and sold for breaking up in November 1921.

In the Mediterranean in 1917.

Acheron Class Destroyer, I Class from 1913

Vickers Ltd., Barrow-in-Furness
Laid down: 4th January 1911; Launched: 9th October 1911; Completed: May 1912
Displacement: 765 tons (norm.), c.990 tons (deep load)
Length: 246 ft 0 in; Beam: 25 ft 8 in; Draught: 9ft 0 in.
Power: Three-shaft Parsons turbines; 13,500 shp - 27 knots. 3 Yarrow boilers.
Oil: 178 tons. Endurance: 1,620 nm at 15 knots.
Armament: 2 x 4-inch; 2 x 12-pdr; 2 x 21-inch torpedo tubes.
Complement: 70

She was in the 1st Destroyer Flotilla when war broke out and it became part of the Grand Fleet. She was with them in the early action on 28th August at Heligoland Bight. From spring 1916 she was attached to the 3rd Battle Squadron, and from October to February 1917 was with the 6th Flotilla, Dover Patrol. After a spell at Portsmouth, she went out to the Mediterranean. On 14th May 1918 she was one of a group of destroyers supporting the Otranto Barrage drifters. Despite zigzagging at 16 knots, she was hit amidships on the starboard side by a torpedo fired by the Austrian submarine *U-27*. Immediately stopped with severe damage, she listed 30 degrees; the Royal Australian Navy destroyer *Warrego* took her in tow and then passed her to an Italian tug. A trawler went alongside to assist but the list increased to 50 degrees so the remainder of the crew were taken off; she rolled over and later sank. Two men were lost.

Creosol Class Fleet Oiler

Tyne Iron Shipbuilding Co.Ltd., Newcastle
Launched: 5th April 1916
Displacement: 2,200 tons.
Length: 210 ft 0 in (pp); Beam: 34 ft 9 in; Draught: 12 ft 0 in.
Power: Triple expansion engine; 700 ihp - 12 knots.

As coal gave way increasingly to oil, large numbers of fleet oilers were built to distribute the new fuel. There was no equipment in use for replenishment at sea as yet, so warships still had to return to port, or anchorage, for alongside refuelling. These were ships which gave long service in many instances. *Philol* lasted until 1956 when she became a hulk but was not finally disposed of until 1967.

Swan, Hunter & Wigham Richardson, Wallsend on Tyne
Launched: 14th September 1916; Completed: January 1917
Displacement: 8,350 tons.
Length: 378 ft 0 in; Beam: 45 ft 6 in; Draught: 22 ft 0 in.
Power: Triple expansion engine; 2,000 ihp - 10 knots.
Armament: 3 x 3 pdr.

She was a larger ship, built for the Royal Australian Navy and entrusted with a token armament. She too had a good length of service, being sold into civilian ownership in 1946 and renamed *Angeliki*.

M15 – M28 Class Monitor

William Gray & Co.Ltd., West Hartlepool
Laid down: March 1915; Launched: 28th April 1915; Completed: June 1915
Displacement: 650 tons (deep load)
Power: Two-shaft, vertical triple expansion engines; 800 ihp – 11 knots. 2 boilers. Oil: 32 tons.
Endurance: 660 naut. miles at 9½ knots.
(for other data, see *M28* page 57)

She was numerically the first of this smaller class of monitors to appear and, on completion, was towed, unarmed, to Malta in July 1915. On arrival in the Dockyard she was fitted with her 9.2-inch gun and mounting. When ready she was sent to Mudros to join the bombardments of Turkish positions in the Gallipoli campaign. After the evacuation from Cape Helles in January 1916, she went to Egypt and took part in the defence of the Suez Canal and supporting the land campaign in Palestine. During this period her shooting was highly praised by Commander Samson of *Ben-My-Chree*, who said that with aerial spotting she was able to get quickly on target and continue to pour in shots, even at her maximum range of 12 miles. When the coastal bombardments were concluded after the Turkish forces had withdrawn beyond the range of the guns, the ships went to the net-protected anchorage of Deir el Belah (Gaza). In the afternoon of 11th November 1917, the German submarine *UC-38* penetrated the net defence and fired torpedoes. One of these hit *M15* on the port side close to the forward magazine; a cordite fire started which caused a partial magazine explosion; the ship broke in two and sank in less than three minutes with the loss of 26 men. Another of the torpedoes fired in this bold attack hit and sank the destroyer *Staunch.*

Centaur Class Cruiser

Sir W.G. Armstrong, Whitworth & Co.Ltd., High Walker
Laid down: 1st February 1915; Launched: 1st April 1916; Completed: December 1916
Displacement: 4,165 tons (norm.), 4,870 tons (deep load)
Length: 446 ft 0 in; Beam: 42 ft 0 in; Draught: c. 14 ft 0 in.
Power: Four-shaft Parsons turbines; 40,000 shp - 29 knots. 6 Yarrow boilers. Oil: 824 tons.
Armament: 5 x 6-inch; 2 x 3-inch AA; 1 x 13-pdr (later replaced by 2 x 2-pdr PomPoms);
2 x 21-inch torpedo tubes.
Armour: Belt 3 - 1¼ inch; Deck: 1 inch; Conning Tower: 6 inch.
Complement: 437

On completion she joined the 5th Light Cruiser Squadron, Harwich Force and remained with them until March 1919. Postwar she served on overseas stations; with the 3rd LCS, Mediterranean Fleet 1919-24; 3rd Cruiser Squadron, Mediterranean Fleet 1924-5, attached to the Australian Station 1925 and China Station 1925-6, then back to 3rd CS 1926-7. A period in reserve was followed by trooping to China in 1928 and then she came back home to join the Signals School at Portsmouth. She paid-off for the last time in January 1933 and was sold for breaking up in August 1935.

*In October 1917 wearing one of the experimental dazzle-paint schemes devised by the artist, and RNVR offi-
cer, Norman Wilkinson. Half-a-dozen warships of different types were chosen to receive such a pattern, and
she was the first battleship.*

Royal Sovereign/Revenge Class Battleship

William Beardmore & Co. Ltd., Dalmuir
Laid down: 12th November 1913; Launched: 12th September 1916; Completed: September 1917
Displacement: 30,400 tons (norm), 33,570 tons (deep load)
Length: 620 ft 7 in; Beam: 88 ft 6 in, hull; 101 ft 6 in over bulges; Draught: 30 ft 0 in (norm), 33 ft 7 in (deep)
Power: Four-shaft Parsons turbines; 40,000 shp - 22 knots. 18 Babcock and Wilcox boilers. Oil: 900/3,400 tons.
Coal for heating and cooking only: 140 tons. Endurance: c.6800 nm at 10 knots.
Armament: 8 x 15-inch; 14 x 6-inch; 2 x 3-inch AA; 4 x 3-pdr; 4 x 21-inch torpedo tubes.
Armour: Belt: 13 - 1 inch; Deck: 4 - 1 inch; Turret: 13 – 4 ½ inch; Barbette: 10 - 4 inch;
Conning tower: 11 - 3 inch.
Complement: 936 in 1917

While building, her hull design was altered to include anti-torpedo bulges. Because of this, her weight on the
slip was greater than usual which, at her launching, caused her rudder and keel plating to be damaged. She was
towed to Cammell Laird for repairs which were carried out in Gladstone Dock, Liverpool. She joined the 1st
Battle Squadron, Grand Fleet in September 1917. Postwar she was in the Atlantic Fleet, with detachments to
the Mediterranean in 1920 and 1922. Later she was with the Mediterranean and Home Fleets, served throughout the Second World War and was finally sold for breaking up in February 1948.

An interestingly posed photograph with her company on display and all looking at the camera! She was a steam yacht of 323 gross tons, built in 1908 for an unknown owner. She was hired for patrol duties on 12th March 1915 and armed with one 12-pdr and one 3-pdr. She was purchased in March 1919 and, in 1922, sold to the newly independent Irish Government and renamed *Muirchu*.

In late 1917, with an aircraft flying-off platform on B turret only; note the Sopwith 1 ½ - strutter in position, but with the platform planking over the gun barrels not in place. Later, a second platform was fitted on X turret.

Queen Elizabeth Class Battleship

John Brown & Co.Ltd., Clydebank
Laid down: 24th February 1913; Launched: 31st December 1914; Completed: October 1915
Displacement: 29,150 tons (norm. by 1917); 33,000 tons (deep load)
Length: 643 ft 9 in: Beam: 90 ft 7½ in; Draught: 29 ft 6 in (norm.), 33 ft 0 in (deep)
Power: Four-shaft Brown-Curtis turbines; 56,000 shp (norm.) - 23 knots, 75,000 shp (overload) - 25 knots.
24 Yarrow boilers.
Oil: 650/3,400 tons. Coal for heating and cooking: 100 tons.
Endurance: 4,500 nm at 15 knots; 6,450 nm at 10 knots.
Armament: 8 x 15-inch; 14 x 6-inch (later; two replaced by 2 x 3-inch AA); 4 x 3-pdr; 4 x 21-inch torpedo tubes.
Armour: Belt: 13 - 4 inch; Deck: 3 - 1 inch; Turret: 13 - 4¼ inch; Barbette: 10 - 4 inch;
Conning tower: 11 - 3 inch
Complement: c.950 originally, 1,016 in 1916

Commissioned in August 1915, she joined the 5th Battle Squadron, Grand Fleet, as flagship in October. In December she was in collision with *Warspite* while on exercises; repairs at Cromarty and Invergordon took two weeks. At Jutland she was hit six times, with two of the hits causing serious damage; she remained in action, and on return, went immediately for repairs which took a month. Postwar she became flagship of the 1st Battle Squadron, Atlantic Fleet in 1920, and in 1924 was with the Mediterranean Fleet. She was partially modernized in 1930 -33. She served in the Second World War until being sunk by *U-331* off Sollum on 25th November 1941.

*In the 2nd Battle Squadron, following **Erin** into a 90° turn to starboard, in late 1917 or early 1918.*
***Agincourt**'s aft pole mast has been removed and a topmast fitted to the derrick-pole amidships. The search-*
lights are on a group of towers around the aft funnel.

(*Service career notes continued from page 68*)

She joined the 2nd Battle Squadron in late 1917 and remained there until the end of the war. In March 1919 she went into reserve at Rosyth and a year later was reduced to care & maintenance only. She was recommissioned in 1921 for experimental work and then stripped for a proposed conversion to a 'Mobile Naval Base', a euphemism for a large depot ship. This was never completed and she was sold for breaking up in December 1922.

(Service career notes continued from page 19)

In 1917, during a refit in Malta, her funnels were raised in an attempt to reduce smoke interference on the bridge. From 1916 she had alternated with **Lord Nelson** between Salonika and Mudros as the only battleships available (apart from one elderly French ship) should **Goeben** attempt to break out. When this did occur, on 20th January 1918, **Agamemnon** was in Mudros when **Goeben** and **Breslau** attacked Imbros, sinking the monitors **Raglan** and **M28**. The Turkish-German ships then intended to attack Mudros to wreak further destruction. **Agamemnon** got underway to intercept the marauders, as seen in this photograph, making an impressive sight as she left. However, no shots were fired because attacks on the enemy were made by RNAS aircraft. Although only small bombs were dropped, they were effective, because, while evading them, the two ships ran into an extensive Allied minefield, in which **Breslau** was sunk and **Goeben** damaged. When the Armistice was agreed with Turkey, the formalities were concluded when the documents were signed on board **Agamemnon** in Mudros Bay on the 30th October 1918. On her return home, after four years' remarkable service in the eastern Mediterranean, she was somewhat ignominiously reduced to the role of a target ship. The conversion was carried out at Chatham between June 1919 and July 1921. She served thus until 1926, when **Centurion** took over, and was then sold for breaking up in January 1927.

C Class Submarine

Vickers Ltd., Barrow-in-Furness
Launched: 3rd October 1906
Displacement: 280 tons (surface), 316 tons (submerged)
Length: 142 ft 2 in; Beam: 13 ft 6 in; Draught: 11 ft 6 in.
Power: Single-shaft, Vickers 16-cylinder petrol engine; 600 hp - 13½ knots, Electric motor; 300 hp - 7½ knots.
Range: 1,000 nm at 8¾ knots (surface)
Armament: 2 x 18-inch torpedo tubes (4 torpedoes carried).
Complement: 16

This mysterious-looking object is the submarine *C3*, in Dover harbour, being prepared for the attack at Zeebrugge in April 1918. Her conning tower is shrouded and a tarpaulin is rigged over the torpedo loading hatch to conceal the proceedings while five tons of explosives are placed in position to carry out her purpose. She was to be taken under the landward end of the mole where a viaduct connected the masonry structure to the shore. Here the charge would be detonated to sever the link and prevent German reinforcements being brought up. Of all the elements of this famous raid, this was the only one which was carried out with complete success. Her crew of six were injured by defending fire but succeeded in getting clear after the fuses had been lit, and were picked up and brought safely home. All received recognition for this outstanding attack - the commander, Lt.R.D. Sandford, was awarded the Victoria Cross; the second-in-command, Lt.J. Howell-Price, the Distinguished Service Order; P.O.Cox.W. Harner, E.R.A. A. Roxburgh, Stoker H. Bendall and leading Seaman W. Cleaver, the Conspicuous Gallantry Medal.

Thornycroft R class destroyer

J.I. Thornycroft & Co.Ltd., Woolston
Laid down: December 1915; Launched: 5th November 1916; Completed: February 1917
Displacement: 1,035 tons
Length: 274 ft 3 in; Beam: 27 ft 3 in; Draught: 9 ft 0 in.
Power: Two-shaft Brown-Curtis turbines; 29,000 shp - 35 knots. 3 Yarrow boilers. Oil: 296 tons.
Armament: 3 x 4-inch; 1 x 2-pdr; 4 x 21-inch torpedo tubes.
Complement: 82

She joined the Harwich Force on completion. One regular duty which the destroyers of this group performed was to provide an escort for the merchant ships operating the 'Beef Trip'. This was the trade link across the North Sea to neutral Holland, bringing back supplies of meat and produce to Britain. On one such trip on the 22/23rd December 1917, a terrible disaster befell the escort. There were eight destroyers that night, and unbeknownst to them, an extensive new minefield had been laid by German destroyers to the west of the Maas light buoy. Late on the night of the 22nd, *Valkyrie* was damaged by a mine and had to be towed by *Sylph*. Then, in the dark early hours of the 23rd, *Torrent*, *Surprise* and *Tornado* all struck mines and sank within 15 minutes. *Radiant*, by good fortune, managed to avoid the mines and picked up the pitifully few survivors, 74 out of 314 men of the three ships' companies. In September 1920 *Radiant* was sold to Siam and renamed *Phra Ruang*.

Probably off the coast near Harwich and in pristine, post refit, condition after being damaged in the attack in July 1918.

C Class Submarine

Vickers Ltd., Barrow-in-Furness
Launched: 10th March 1909

(for Boats' data notes, see *C3* page 110)

The most famous event in this boat's life was the mistaken addition of her destruction to the victory tally of a noted German air ace. This was Kpt.Lt. Friedrich Christiansen who, on the 6th July 1918, led a group of seaplanes from Zeebrugge Naval Air Station in a raid on Lowestoft. On their return they surprised *C25* on the surface off Orfordness and immediately attacked. Machine-gun fire killed the commander and fatally injured three other men on the conning tower. Two more of the crew were killed trying to clear the bodies from the hatch but the boat could not drive as the pressure hull had been pierced in numerous places. *E51* came upon the scene and tried to help but had to dive herself to avoid an attack by more seaplanes summoned by wireless by the first group. The destroyer *Lurcher* finally succeeded in driving the aircraft off and *C25* was towed back to Harwich. Although she was repaired, the Germans' belief that she had been sunk has oft been repeated, even recently, as fact. Actually, she was sold for breaking up in December 1921.

Yarrow M Class Destroyer

Yarrow & Co., Scotstoun
Laid down: 18th October 1914; Launched: 23rd April 1915; Completed: June 1915
Displacement: 895 tons
Length: 271 ft 6 in; Beam: 26 ft 0 in; Draught: 9ft 6 in.
Power: Two-shaft Brown-Curtis turbines; 23,000 shp - 35 knots. 3 Yarrow boilers. Oil: 254 tons.
Armament: 3 x 4-inch; 1 x 2-pdr; 4 x 21-inch torpedo tubes.
Complement: 80

Other than that she carried out the usual destroyer duties, no details are available of her life, except that, in 1918, she was with the Harwich Force as seen here. She went to the breakers in May 1921.

Modified R Class Destroyer

William Beardmore & Co.Ltd., Dalmuir
Laid down: 19th June 1916; Launched: 10th October 1917; Completed: November 1917
Displacement: 975 tons (norm.), 1,173 tons (deep load)
Length: 276 ft 0 in; Beam: 26 ft 8 in; Draught: 9 ft (norm.), 11 ft (deep)
Power: Two-shaft Brown-Curtis turbines; 27,000 shp - 36 knots. 3 Yarrow boilers. Oil: 296 tons.
Armament: 3 x 4-inch; 1 x 2-pdr; 4 x 21-inch torpedo tubes.
Complement: 82

Likewise with this ship, little is known of her service, but as she came later on the scene, within a year of the wars's end, this is the less surprising. It is believed that this photograph was also taken at Harwich. One point of detail interest is the after 4-inch gun being on the R class bandstand type mounting, whereas *Moon* has the earlier deck level mounting of the gun. *Ulster* was sold for breaking up in April 1928.

Off St. Michael's Mount in 1918. The white bands on the casing were for identification by friendly aircraft.

C Class Submarine

H.M. Dockyard, Chatham
Launched: 13th August 1908
(for Boats' data notes, see *C3* page 110)

She was the first Royal Navy submarine not built by Vickers. In August 1914 she was with the 4th Flotilla at Dover and in 1916-17, the 5th Flotilla, Dover, sometimes operating from Dunkirk. In May 1917 she was sunk in collision with **Lurcher**, but was raised , repaired and refitted at Chatham and returned to service to gain another first. She was the first boat to carry out a submarine beach reconnaissance. She lay on the bottom for 36 hours off Middlekerke, Belgium, to measure the rise-and-fall of the tide, using her depth gauge to measure the tidal depth range. This was a part of preparations for a planned amphibious assault on the coast in support of the Army's third offensive at Ypres. The long period on the bottom, unable to ventilate the boat, led to foul air conditions which badly effected the crew - so it was unfortunate that the amphibious plan came to nothing! In early 1918 she went to the 6th Flotilla at Dolphin (Gosport), and between February and May, was on experimental duties at Portland. She was sold for breaking up in November 1919.

Humber Class River Monitor

Vickers Ltd., Barrow-in-Furness
Laid down: 24th August 1912; Launched: 17th June 1913; Completed: November 1913
Displacement: 1,520 tons (deep load)
Length: 266 ft 9 in; Beam: 49 ft 0 in; Draught: 5 ft 7½ in.
Power: Two-shaft, triple expansion engines; 1,450 ihp - 9½ knots. 2 Yarrow boilers. Coal: 187 tons.
Oil: 90 tons. Endurance: 1,650 nm at 8 knots, coal only; 2,800 nm at 8 knots, on coal and oil.
Armament: 2 x 6-inch; (3 x 6-inch From 1915); 2 x 4.7-inch howitzers; 4 x 3-pdr; six or seven Hotchkiss
machine guns.
Armour: Belt: 3 - 1½ inch; Turret face: 4 inch; Barbette: 3½ inch.
Complement: 140

Built for Brazil as the river monitor *Javary* but laid up at Barrow when Brazil was unable to pay. In August 1914 she was bought for the Royal Navy and prepared for service. She was at Dover by the end of the month and on Belgian Coast operations in October and November. In March 1915 she went to the Mediterranean with her sisters and in company with the liner *Trent*. In June 1915 she was at Gallipoli. She had a refit, including new guns, at Alexandria in January 1916 and remained in Egyptian waters. She was guardship at Aqaba from August 1917 to February 1918 and in October, went to Mudros with her sisters. Post-Armistice, she spent three months at Constantinople and returned home in March 1919. She was refitted at Devonport and left for Murmansk on 20th May; returned home, under tow, in September and was paid-off the following month at Chatham. She was sold in 1920 to the Dutch salvage company F. Rijsdijk and converted into a crane barge.

TB13-36 Class Torpedo Boat (Coastal Destroyer)

R. &W. Hawthorn, Leslie & Co.Ltd., Hebburn on Tyne
Laid down: 7th February 1908; Launched: 22nd February 1909; Completed: August 1910

(For class data notes, see *TB15* page 35)

Although *TB34* has left little in the records, this photograph is of interest because it shows another task such ships might be called upon to carry out. She is towing an RNAS (or RAF) Short 184 seaplane. No details of the particular occasion are known but it was a quite frequent occurrence for seaplanes to land with engine trouble and need such assistance. The problem might be due to a blocked fuel pipe or an oil leak or damage from enemy fire. If emergency repairs could not be made by the crew, then a tow would be needed. This was not an easy job and would need reasonable weather conditions – the aircraft could not be towed at speed as the float supporting structure might collapse, leading to loss of the machine or severe damage at best. Conditions here look good and TB34 is about to get underway, so we might assume that this one was returned successfully to base. TB34 was scrapped in 1921.

K8, *K15* and *K6* alongside *Royal Arthur* at Rosyth, 1918

Some interesting details of the K class boats are shown here; particulary the funnels and the way in which they were retracted prior to diving. On *K6*, in the foreground, can be seen the well into which the funnel would be folded aft on the hinged pivots attached to each side.Forward of the funnel, lying flat, is the circular plate which would be folded aft to seal the boiler uptake, once the funnel itself had been lowered. Note that the forefunnel hinged forwards. The position of the two 4-inch guns is shown as is the 'swan bow' which was developed to improve sea-keeping qualities when running on the surface. *Royal Arthur* was an Edgar class cruiser which, after being withdrawn, in 1915, from the 10th Cruiser Squadron on the Northern Patrol was converted into a submarine depot ship. In 1918 she was operating with the 12th Submarine Flotilla and, postwar, with the 1st Flotilla, until being paid-off in December 1920.

(For K class data notes, see *K5* page 91)

K6   H.M. Dockyard, Devonport; Launched: 31st May 1916; Sold for breaking up in July 1926

K8   Vickers Ltd., Barrow-in-Furness; Launched: 10th October 1916; Sold for breaking up in October 1923. (*K8* had Parsons turbines)

K15   Scott's Shipbuilding & Engineering Co. Ltd., Greenock; Launched: 31st October 1917; Sold for breaking up in August 1924

Scott Class Flotilla Leader

Cammell Laird & Co.Ltd., Birkenhead
Laid down: 12th May 1917; Launched: 26th February 1918; Completed: May 1918
Displacement: 1,580 tons (norm.), 2,050 tons (deep load)
Length: 332 ft 6 in; Beam: 31 ft 9 in; Draught: 12 ft 6 in.
Power: Two-shaft Parsons turbines; 40,000 shp - 36 knots.
4 Yarrow boilers. Oil: 500 tons. Endurance: 3,390 nm at 15 knots.
Armament: 5 x 4.7-inch; 1 x 3-inch AA; 2 x 2-pdr PomPoms; 6 x 21-inch torpedo tubes.
Complement: 164

Bruce joined the 10th Destroyer Flotilla at Harwich for the last months of the war. Post-war she went to the China Station, becoming the leader of the 4th Submarine Flotilla. She returned home in 1937 and went into reserve. After this, she became a target ship and was expended in that role when she was sunk off the Isle of Wight on 22nd November 1939.

Off the Belgian coast with attendant ML.

Gorgon Class Monitor

Sir W.G. Armstrong, Whitworth & Co.Ltd., Elswick
Laid down: 11th June 1913; Launched: 9th June 1914; Completed: June 1918
Displacement: 4,825 tons (norm.), 5,746 tons (deep load)
Length: 310 ft 0 in; Beam: 55 ft 0 in; 73 ft 7 in over bulges; Draught: 16 ft 4 in.
Power: Two-shaft, vertical triple expansion engines; 4,000 ihp - 12 knots.
4 Yarrow boilers. Coal: 175/364 tons. Oil: 175 tons.
Endurance: c.2,500 nm at 10 knots.
Armament: 2 x 9.2-inch; 4 x 6-inch; 2 x 3-inch AA; 4 x 2-pdr AA.
Armour: Belt :7 - 3 inch; Deck: 2½ - 1 inch; Turret and barbette: 8 - 6 inch; Conning tower: 8 inch.
Complement: 323

She was laid down as *Nidaros*, one of a pair of Coast Defence Battleships for Norway. Construction was suspended in August 1914 until January 1915, when she was converted for the Royal Navy to serve in the monitor role. She commissioned in May 1918 and arrived at Dover in June to join the bombardments of the German batteries on the Belgian coast. On 15th October she fired the last shell of this war-long task. In November she went to Portsmouth while a decision was made about her disposal, then she was used in trials to determine the cause of the loss of her sister *Glatton*, which had been sunk in Dover Harbour after a magazine fire. Resale to Norway did not take place and she went to Devonport in April 1919 to act as a temporary tender to *Vivid*. Paid-off in August, she went into reserve at Devonport. A possible sale to Argentina, Peru or Romania came to nothing, so she was used as a target for bombs and shells. She was finally sold in August 1928 for breaking up.

Type M Kite Balloon

Envelope length: 82 ft 0 in; Diameter: 26 ft 7 in;
Hydrogen gas capacity: c. 18,000 cu.ft.
Normal observation altitude: 1,000 - 1,500 ft.

Arabis Class (Flower Class) Fleet Sweeping Sloop

Workman Clark & Co. Ltd., Belfast
Launched: 5th February 1916
(For class data notes, see *Snapdragon* page 76)

A new type of kite balloon was introduced in 1917 which was a considerable advance over the design of the Type H (see *Manica*). This, the Type M or Caquot type, was of French origin from a design by Captitaine Albert Caquot. It had the considerable advantage of being able to be towed at speeds of 20 knots and in a wind speed up to Force 6. Balloons were inflated in special shore bases and taken by weighted lorries to the quayside for transfer to the ship. Topping up of hydrogen would be carried out from a barge, as is happening here in the photograph, taken in Malta. Further hydrogen bottles were carried on board for topping up while at sea.

Pentstemon was on convoy escort in the Mediterranean from Malta eastwards. Sold in April 1920 she became a merchant ship, at first named *Lila*. She then found her way to Chinese ownership whence, as *Hai Li*, she was purchased in 1932 for conversion to a gunboat and renamed *Hai Chow*. On the 7th October 1937 she was sunk by Japanese aircraft in the estuary of the Pearl River.

Arabis Class (Flower Class) Fleet Sweeping Sloop

Barclay Curle & Co. Ltd., Whiteinch, Glasgow
Launched: 19th February 1916

She was on Western Patrol duties and guarding Atlantic trade routes to the Straits of Gibraltar. She did not last long after the war, going to the breakers in January 1923.

Firing off Ostend with ML smokescreening.

Erebus Class Monitor

Harland & Wolff, Govan
Laid down: 12th October 1915; Launched: 19th June 1916; Completed: September 1916

(For class data notes, see *Terror* page 97)

As with her sister *Terror*, she joined the Monitor Squadron at Dover in September 1916. While off the Belgian coast on the 28th October 1917, she was hit by a German remotely-controlled explosive boat. Damage was repaired within a month and she was back on duty by the 21st November. She remained at Dover until after the Armistice and in January 1919, became tender to the Chatham Gunnery School. She was sent to the White Sea in July 1919 and, in October, was diverted to Copenhagen and supported operations in the Gulf of Finland until the end of the year, reaching Chatham on 31st December. In 1921 she was used in the firing trials against a surrendered German battleship *Baden*. Subsequently paid-off into Care & Maintenance, she next served as a drill-ship until being refitted in 1939 for service throughout the Second World War. She was sold for breaking up in 1946.

Caledon Class Cruiser

Scott's Shipbuilding & Engineering Co.Ltd., Greenock
Laid down: 21st February 1916; Launched: 23rd December 1916; Completed: June 1917
Displacement: 4,120 tons (norm.), 4,950 tons (deep load)
Length: 450 ft |0 in; Beam: 42 ft 9 in; Draught: 14 ft 6 in (norm.), 16 ft 3 in (deep).
Power: Two-shaft Parsons turbines; 40,000 shp - 29 knots.
6 Yarrow Boilers. Oil: 935 tons.
Armament: 5 x 6-inch; 2 x 3-inch AA; 4 x 3-pdr; 8 x 21-inch torpedo tubes.
Armour: Belt: 3 - 1¼ inch; Deck: 1 inch; Conning tower: 6 inch.
Complement: 400

She commissioned for service with the 6th Light Cruiser Squadron, Grand Fleet, in June 1917, this formation later being attached to the Battlecruiser Force. In December 1918 she was in the Baltic and took part in the capture of the Bolshevik destroyers *Avtroil* and *Spartak* off Reval, in company with her sister *Calypso* and V&W class destroyers. (The captured ships were presented to the Estonian Navy and were later sold to Peru). *Caradoc* served from 1919 to 1927 with the 3rd Light Cruiser Squadron in the Mediterranean Fleet with a detachment to China in 1926-27. She was on the North America and West Indies Station 1928-30 and in China 1930-34. She then went into reserve. She served in the Second World War, in 1944 becoming a base ship and was finally sold for breaking up in 1946.

Running full-power trials in the spring of 1918

Admiralty V Class Destroyer

Swan, Hunter & Wigham Richardson, Wallsend on Tyne
Laid down: February 1917; Launched: 29th October 1917; Completed: May 1918
Displacement: c.1,300 tons (norm.), 1,490 tons (deep load)
Length: 312 ft 0 in; Beam: 29 ft 6 in; Draught: 10 ft 9 in (norm.), 11 ft 7 in (deep).
Power: Two-shaft Parsons turbines; 27,000 shp - 34 knots.
3 Yarrow boilers.
Oil: 185 tons (min), 367 tons (max). Endurance: c.3,000 nm at 15 knots
Armament: 4 x 4-inch; 1 x 3-inch AA; 4 x 21-inch torpedo tubes.
Complement: 134

She joined the 11th Destroyer Flotilla at Rosyth. On the night of the 4th/5th November she was secured along-side the depot ship *Blake*, with *Viscount* moored outside her, at eight hours notice for steam. At 0300 the wind veered to westward and rapidly became gale-force. Extra hawsers were passed to allow for the conditions but despite this, an hour later both destroyers broke adrift. A magnificent performance by the engine room staffs of both ships got steam raised in about 70 minutes and they were able to ride out the storm. In December 1918 she was in the 20th Destroyer Flotilla fitted for mine laying. She was in the force sent to safeguard the Baltic States in 1919. On 1st September, at anchor off Seskar Island in the approaches to Petrograd, she was hit by two torpedoes fired by the Bolshvik submarine *Pantera*. She rolled over and sank within five minutes, with the loss of eight men.

In Dockyard Creek, Grand Harbour, Malta in 1918.

M Class Submarine

Vickers Ltd., Barrow-in-Furness
Launched: 9th July 1917; Completed: April 1918
Displacement: 1,594 tons, surface; 1,946 tons, submerged
Length: 295 ft 9 in; Beam: 24 ft 8 in; Draught: 15 ft 11 in.
Power: Two-shaft, Vickers 12-cylinder diesel engines/four electric motors; 2,400/1,600 hp - 15/9 knots.
Oil: 76 tons
Range: 3,840 nm at 10 knots on the surface
Armament: 1 x 12-inch; 1 x 3-inch AA; 4 x 18-inch torpedo tubes
(50 x 12-inch rounds and eight torpedoes carried).
Complement: 65

If the K class submarines were revolutionary, so too were the M class. Four K class boats, as yet unbuilt, were cancelled and the order changed to four boats to a new design. To maintain secrecy they were laid down, in 1916, under the alias of the Ks – *M1* as *K18*. Doubts about the reliability of torpedoes prompted studies into the feasibility of putting a large-calibre gun into a submarine. The principal idea was that the boat would be able to surface and sink its target rapidly with heavy shells, catching the enemy unprepared. A design was drawn up and the boats ordered. By the time the first boat commissioned there were no likely targets so *M1*, after a spell with the 6th and 11th Submarine Flotillas, was dispatched to the Mediterranean in August 1918. Here a plan was made for her to bombard Constantinople and she set off on this venture. She was about to enter the Dardanelles when the operation was cancelled. This was possibly due to the realization, based on previous experience, that for a boat her size it would not be worth the risk of attempting a passage through the nets and minefields and the treacherous currents. *M1* returned home not having fired a shot in anger.

This photograph probably dates from 1919 when *M1* was making test shots and was filmed 'in action'. One round could be loaded prior to the submarine diving so that she could fire seconds after the gun was clear of the surface. After that further rounds could be loaded but this could not be done while the boat was submerged. A detail shown here is that her number is white, shaded black, whereas in the previous picture, taken during the war, it was black, shaded white. *M1* remained in service until she was sunk with all hands in a glancing collision with the merchant ship *Vidar*, which was not aware at the time of what had happened. This occurred on 12th November 1925 off Start Point.

At Brindisi after being torpedoed off Durazzo on 2nd October 1918.

Weymouth Class Cruiser

Sir W.G. Armstrong, Whitworth & Co.Ltd., Elswick
Laid down: 19th January 1910; Launched: 18th November 1910; Completed: April 1912
Displacement: 5,250 (norm.), 5,800 tons (deep load)
Length: 453 ft 0 in; Beam: 48 ft 6 in; Draught: 15 ft 6 in.
Power: Four-shaft Parsons turbines; 22,000 shp - 25 knots.
12 Yarrow boilers.
Coal: 1,290 tons. Oil: 260 tons. Endurance: c.4,500 nm at 10 knots.
Armament: 8 x 6-inch; 1 x 3-inch AA; 4 x 3-pdr; 2 x 21-inch torpedo tubes.
Armour: Deck: 2 - ¾ inch; Conning tower: 4 inch.
Complement:475

At the outbreak of war she was in the 2nd Light Cruiser Squadron, Mediterranean Fleet. In August 1914 she was sent to the Indian Ocean to hunt for *Emden* and then to East Africa for the operations against *Konigsberg* in the Rufiji River, February to July 1915. In December 1915 she went to the Adriatic and then returned home to joint the 6th Light Cruiser Squadron, Grand Fleet in 1916 - 1917; she was detached to Bermuda in December 1916. From 1917 - 19 she was based at Brindisi with the 8th LCS and was damaged by torpedo from the Austrian submarine *U-28*. She paid-off at Malta and was refitted to join the 7th LCS, South America Station between March 1920 and January 1921. She went into reserve at the Nore from July 1921 until December 1925 and was then flagship, Vice-Admiral, Nore Reserve until being finally paid-off into the dockyard control at Portsmouth in September 1927. Placed on the sales list in 1928, she was sold for breaking up in October that year.

As a minelayer in 1918.

London Class Battleship

H.M. Dockyard, Portsmouth
Laid down: 8th December 1898; Launched: 21st September 1899; Completed: June 1902
Displacement: 14,500 ton (norm.), 15,700 tons (deep load)
Length: 431 ft 9 in; Beam: 75 ft 0 in; Draught: 26 ft 6 in.
Power: Two-shaft, 3 cylinder triple expansion engines; 15,000 ihp - 18 knots.
20 Belleville boilers
Coal: 900 tons (min), 2,000 tons (max)
Endurance: 3,000 nm at 10 knots.
Armament: 4 x 12-inch; 12 x 6-inch; 16 x 12-pdr; 6 x 3-pdr; 4 x 18-inch torpedo tubes.
Armament as minelayer: 3 x 6-inch; 1 x 4-inch; 240 mines.
Armour: Belt: 9 - 3 inch; Deck: 2½ - 1 inch; Turret: 10 - 8 inch; Barbette: 12 - 6 inch; Conning tower: 14 inch.
Complement: c.800; 481 as minelayer

In 1914 she was in the 5th Battle Squadron. From August she was on Channel Patrols and then went to the Dardanelles in March 1915 to replace losses. In May 1915 she was sent to the Adriatic to strengthen Italian forces and remained, based at Taranto, until 1917. She returned home and underwent conversion to a minelayer at Rosyth Dockyard. Completed thus, on the 8th May 1918, she joined the 1st Minelaying Squadron at Grangemouth. In the conversion the 12-inch guns were removed from the forward turret. The after turret and barbette were removed and replaced by a 6-inch gun, and the entire main deck aft was converted to the mine deck with rails for 240 mines. In 1919 she was a reserve depot ship and was sold for breaking up in June 1920.

Also with the 1st Minelaying Squadron and seen on the same occasion as the previous photograph.

Launched: 1914
5,934 gross tons
Length: 395 ft 6 in; Beam: 54 ft 0 in; Draught: 16 ft 10 in.
Power: Two-shaft turbines; 15,000 shp - 22½ knots. Oil: 585 tons.
Armament: 2 x 4.7-inch; 2 x 12-pdr; 2 x 6-pdr AA; 1 x 2-pdr PomPom; 500 mines
Complement: 215

She was a Canadian Pacific Railway coastal passenger ship for the Vancouver to Seattle route, hired at the outbreak of war for conversion as a minelayer. She was fitted out by Denny and entered service on 26th December 1914. During the war she laid 25,242 mines, more than any other converted merchant ship minelayer. She was purchased on 14th June 1919 and was involved with the Baltic campaign of that year. She was eventually sold for breaking up in May 1929.

With a Sopwith Camel on her aircraft platform in 1918.

Chatham Class Cruiser

Cammell Laird & Co.Ltd., Birkenhead
Laid down: 14th April 1911; Launched: 30th May 1912; Completed: January 1913
Displacement: 5,400 tons (norm.), 6,000 tons (deep load).
Length: 458 ft 0 in; Beam: 49 ft 0 in; Draught: 16 ft 0 in.
Power: Four-shaft Parsons turbines; 25,000 shp - 25½ knots.
12 Yarrow boilers
Coal: 1,240 tons. Oil: 260 tons. Endurance: c.4,500 nm at 16 knots
Armament: 8 x 6-inch; 1 x 3-pdr in AA; 4 x 3-pdr; 2 x 21-inch torpedo tubes.
Armour: Belt: 2 inch on 1 inch plating; Deck: 1½ - 3/8 inch; Conning tower: 4 inch.
Complement: 475

She was in the Pacific in 1913 – 14 and, when war broke out, was sent to the North America and West Indies Station until 1916. In that year she came to British waters to join the 2nd Light Cruiser Squadron, Grand Fleet, until the Armistice. In 1918 she was fitted with a revolving platform for a Sopwith Camel. On the 1st June 1918 she was with a force sent to attack German naval forces protecting minesweepers in the Heligoland Bight. When German seaplanes were spotted, she and *Sydney* flew off their Camels to intercept them but the results were inconclusive. In March 1919 she left Spithead for Australia in company with the destroyers *Huon*, *Parramatta*, *Warrego* and *Yarra*. She relieved *Sydney* as Flagship, Royal Australian Navy, in October 1927 until February 1928 and then left for the U.K. where she paid-off at Portsmouth in April and was sold for breaking up in December 1928.

Sir W.G. Armstrong, Whitworth & Co.Ltd., High Walker
Laid down: 8th June 1915; Launched: 15th August 1916; Completed: July 1917
Displacement: 19,513 tons (norm.), 22,890 tons (deep load.)
Length: 786 ft 9 in; Beam: 88 ft 0 in; Draught: 21 ft 6 in (norm.), 24 ft 0 in (deep)
Power: Four-shaft Brown-Curtis geared turbines: 94,000 shp - 31½ knots.
18 Yarrow boilers. Oil: 750 tons (min.), 3,393 tons (max.).
Endurance: 6,000 nm at 20 knots.
Armament: 1 x 18-inch (designed for two); 11 x 5.5-inch; 2 x 3-inch AA; 2 x 3-pdr; 18 x 21-inch torpedo
tubes (incl. Two submerged), later reduced to six (4 and 2).
Armour: Belt: 3 - 2 inch; Deck: 3 - ¾ inch; Turret: 11 - 4¼ inch; Barbette: 7 - 4 inch;
Conning tower: 10 - 3 inch.
Complement: 880 in 1917, 932 in 1918 (incl. Aviation personnel)

As aircraft carrier:

Armament: 10 x 5.5-inch; 6 x 3-inch AA;
Nominal aircraft complement: 16 in 1918, 10 before full conversion.
Forward hangar: 64 ft x 36 ft; Take-off deck: 228 ft x 50 ft (max).
Aft Hangar: 70 ft x 38 ft; landing deck: 284 ft x 70 ft.
Electrically powered lifts 48 ft x 18 ft, one forward and one aft.

Building as a sister ship to **Courageous** and **Glorious** but with an experimental armament of 18-inch guns, **Furious** became the Royal Navy's most important aircraft carrier of the war. The forward 18-inch gun turret and barbette was replaced by a hangar with a flying-off deck extending to the bow. She joined the Grand Fleet in July 1917 and carried out trials until November. As a result of these it was decided to build a second, landing, deck aft of the funnel. Conversion began in December and she was ready to recommission at Rosyth on 15th March 1918 for the Flying Squadron of the Grand Fleet, this being about the time of the photograph. She became flagship of R.Adm. Phillimore, Admiral Commanding Aircraft. Landing trials with Sopwith Pups began in April but were fraught with difficulties, often ending with aircraft getting entangled in the rope barrier aft of the funnel, or going over the side. Landings were suspended but the flying-off deck continued to be used, aircraft either landing ashore or ditching near destroyers when at sea. **Furious**, her aircraft and their pilots achieved three outstanding 'firsts' in naval aviation:-

2nd August 1917 – in Scapa Flow, Squadron Commander E.H. Dunning made the first successful deck landing on a ship underway in Sopwith Pup N6453. On the 7th , in the same aircraft, a second successful landing was made but on the same day, on the third landing attempt in N6452, the aircraft went over the side and Dunning was tragically drowned.

19th June 1918 - a reconnaissance mission off the Danish coast was attacked by seaplanes flying from Sylt. Two Camels were flown off and one of the pilots, Lt.G. Heath, shot down a Friedrichshafen FF49C, the first victory for a carrier-borne fighter.

19th July 1918 – The first successful carrier-borne strategic air strike was made against the German airship station at Tondern, in Schleswig. Seven Camels, each with two 50lb bombs, took off and flew the 80 miles to bomb the sheds, with the result being the destruction of the Zeppelins L54 and L60. Three Camels returned to ditch near destroyers and the pilots were picked up, three landed in Denmark and one was lost without trace.

Furious went to the Baltic in 1919 until November, when she went into reserve. Conversion into a full-deck aircraft carrier was made between 1922 and 1925. She served in the Second World War and was sold for breaking up in January 1948.

In Scapa Flow, with aircraft platforms on A and Y turrets, 1918.

Glorious/Courageous, Class Cruiser

Harland & Wolff, Belfast
Laid down: 1st May 1915: Launched: 20th April 1916; Completed: January 1917
Displacement: 19,180 tons (norm), 22,560 tons (deep load)
Length: 786 ft 9 in; Beam: 81 ft 0 in; Draught: 22 ft 8 in (norm.), 25 ft 10 in (deep.)
Power: Four-shaft Parsons geared turbines; 90,000 shp - 32 knots. 18 Yarrow boilers.
Oil: 750/3,160 tons. Endurance: 6,000 nm at 20 knots.
Armament: 4 x 15-inch; 18 x 4-inch; 2 x 3-inch AA; 2 x 3-pdr;
14 x 21-inch torpedo tubes (incl. Two submerged)
Armour: Belt: 3-2 inch; Deck: 3-1 inch; Turret: 11- 4¼ inch; Barbette: 7-3 inch; Conning tower: 10-3 inch.
Complement: 768

She and her sister were good-looking, well-proportioned ships but their design concept was seriously flawed. They were intended for an ambitious, over-optimistic scheme, a brainchild of Admiral Jackie Fisher, to support an amphibious assault on the Baltic coast of Germany. This was entirely impractical with the technology available, and with the evidence provided by the experience of the Gallipoli landings, never came near to fruition. As a result, the two ships ended up as misfits with no clear role. They were strictly large light cruisers but their size, and main armament calibre, meant that they were treated as battlecruisers; and here they were at a disadvantage with only four 15-inch guns. However, they were constructed and had to be used. In January 1917, *Glorious* joined the 2nd Light Cruiser Squadron, Grand Fleet, as flagship, and saw action in a skirmish with German light forces in the Heligoland Bight on 17th November 1917. In January 1918 she was with the 1st LCS, Battlecruiser Force and remained there until the end of the war. In 1919 she was attached to the gunnery school at Devonport and then became flagship of the Reserve. Between 1924 and 1930 she underwent transformation into an aircraft carrier. She was controversially sunk, with heavy loss of life, by the German battlecruisers *Scharnhorst* and *Gneisenau* off Norway on the 8th June 1940.

Anchored off Rosyth, 1918

William Beardmore & Co.Ltd., Dalmuir
Laid down: June 1914; Launched: 2nd December 1917; Completed: September 1918
Displacement: 15,775 tons (norm.), 16,500 tons (deep load)
Length: 566 ft 0 in; Beam: 68 ft 0 in; Draught: 21 ft 0 in.
Power: Four-shaft Parsons turbines; 20,000 shp - 20 knots. 12 boilers.
Oil: 2,000 tons. Endurance: 4,370 nm at 16 knots.
Armament: 4 x 4-inch AA; 2 x 4-inch LA.
Flight deck: 550 ft x 68 ft, Hangar: 350 ft x 68 ft max.
Forward lift: 30 ft x 36 ft; Aft lift: 60 ft x 18 ft.
Aircraft complement: up to 20 Sopwith T1 Cuckoo torpedo carriers.
Complement: 495 in 1918

A liner being built for the Italian Lloyd Sabaudo Line, to be named ***Conte Rosso***, had work stopped on the out-break of war only two months after being laid down. For two years she lay on the stocks until being bought for the Admiralty for completion as a purpose-designed flight-deck aircraft carrier. Not completed until September 1918, she was too late to see any action but, after commissioning at Glasgow that month, she was soon active with her aircraft. With Sopwith 1½ Strutters the first landings-on and take-offs were made on 24th September 1918. She joined the Flying Squadron, Grand Fleet, and her Sopwith Cuckoos began to come aboard just as the war ended. From 1919 she was with the Atlantic Fleet. She served throughout the Second World War, mainly for deck-landing training and on aircraft ferrying trips, especially to Malta. She was sold for breaking up in December 1946.

In the Mediterranean in 1918

Caledon Shipbuilding & Engineering Co.Ltd., Dundee
Launched: April 1917
1,586 gross tons
Length: 270 ft 4 in (pp); Beam: 37 ft 9 in; Draught: 17 ft 4 in.
Power: Single-shaft, 3 cylinder triple expansion engine; 1,800 ihp.
Armament: 3 x 4-inch.

Laid down as **Goodwin**, a passenger-cargo ship for the Clyde Shipping Company of Glasgow, on completion she was acquired for service as a Q-ship or Decoy Vessel. She operated from Buncrana on the north coast of Ireland under various names; **Ballantrae**, **Moderley** and **Underwing**. By the 13th May 1918 she was on convoy duty in the Mediterranean and saw the war out there. In May 1919 she was returned to her owners to take up her intended trading duties. She was in service again during the Second World War, including two years, from 1943 to 1945, as a convoy rescue ship.

One of **Underwing**'s 4-inch MKVII BL guns with gun's crew in ' merchant-seamens attire'. It is not clear where her guns were mounted, but this one might have been in the 'deckhouse' on the poop.

Launched: 1910
543 gross tons
Speed: 10½ knots.
Armament: 1 x 12-pdr; 1 x 6-pdr AA.

She was a classic example of a steam coaster, hundreds of which carried multifarious cargoes from, and to, ports around Britain and to others across the North Sea and English Channel. *Perdita* was requisitioned as a naval stores carrier from August 1915. She went out to the Mediterranean and worked thus until January the following year. Then she was taken over to increase the minelaying capabilities in the eastern Mediterranean and Aegean Sea. Fitted out at Mudros with mine rails and with her stern bulwarks squared-off and fitted with doors and chutes, she could carry a maximum of 150 mines. Two-thirds of this load were stored below decks and 50 (25 x 2) were carried on the rails ready to lay. She laid 1,332 mines in all and was eventually safely returned to her Liverpool owners in August 1919.

*With **Tiger** in the Firth of Forth in 1918*

Minotaur Class Armoured Cruiser

H.M. Dockyard, Chatham
Laid down: 2nd January 1905; Launched: 20th September 1906; Completed: March 1908
Displacement: 14,600 tons (norm.), 16,100 tons (deep load)
Length: 519 ft 0 in; Beam: 74 ft 6 in; Draught: 26 ft 0 in.
Power: Two-shaft, four-cylinder triple expansion engines; 27,000 ihp - 23 knots.
Coal: 950/2,060 tons. Oil: 750 tons. Endurance: 8,150 nm at 10 knots.
Armament: 4 x 9.2-inch; 10 x 7.5-inch; 16 x 12-pdr; 5 x 18-inch torpedo tubes.
Armour: Belt: 6 - 3 inch; Deck: 1½ - ¾ inch; Turret: 8 - 4½ inch; Barbette: 7 - 3 inch; Conning tower: 10 inch.
Complement: 755

In August 1914 she was in the 2nd Cruiser Squadron, Grand Fleet. She took part in the Battle of Jutland and, in November 1916, went to Murmansk. In 1917 - 18 she operated as an Atlantic convoy escort. Postwar she went into reserve and was then used as an accommodation ship attached to *Actaeon*, the Torpedo School at Sheerness, until finally paying-off in 1922 and being sold for breaking up in December.

At Gibraltar in 1918.

S. McKnight & Co., Ayr
Launched: 2nd December 1889
Displacement: 440 tons. 291 gross tons.
Length: 135 ft 0 in (pp); Beam: 24 ft 0 in; Draught: 12 ft 0 in.
Power: Single-shaft, two-cylinder compound engine; 650 ihp.

She began the war at Gibraltar, having started life as a civilian tug and then being purchased for the Admiralty as early as 28th February 1896. She was launched as *Flying Vulture* for the Clyde Shipping Company. Although classified by the Admiralty as a harbour tug, she was actually equipped for salvage work. She was sold, still at Gibraltar, on 5th November 1924. At the time of this photograph, Temp.Lt. F.C. Poyser RNR was in command. As mentioned in the Introduction, he was one of the founders of the Nautical Photo Agency. Earlier in his sea-going career, in 1912, he had joined T & J.Harrison and was 3rd Officer in *Statesman* when she carried the MLs to Britain as depicted previously (*see page 27*)

Newly commissioned in September 1918

Thornycroft S Class Destroyer

J.I. Thornycroft & Co.Ltd., Woolston
Laid down: May 1917; Launched: 1st June 1918; Completed: August 1918.
Displacement: 1,087 tons (norm.), 1,240 tons (deep load)
Length: 276 ft 0 in; Beam: 27 ft 4 in; Draught: 10 ft 6 in.
Power: Two-shaft Brown-Curtis turbines; 29,000 shp - 36 knots. 3 Yarrow boilers. Oil: 300 tons.
Armament: 3 x 4-inch; 1 x 2-pdr; 4 x 21-inch torpedo tubes, 2 x 18-inch torpedo tubes at break at focsle,
one each port and starboard.
Complement: 90

On completion she joined the Grand Fleet but saw no action by that late date in the war. She only had a short career post-war, being sunk in collision with a merchant ship in the Sea of Mamora on 24th September 1922.

With others of the 4th Battle Squadron steaming out to meet the German ships arriving on 21st November 1918.

H.M. Dockyard, Portsmouth
Laid down: 19th January 1909; Launched: 30th September 1909; Completed: January 1911
Displacement: 19,680 tons (norm.), 23,123 tons (deep load)
Length: 546 ft 0 in; Beam: 85 ft 0 in; Draught: 28ft 6 in.
Power: Four-shaft Parsons turbines; 25,000 shp - 21 knots. 18 Yarrow boilers.
Coal: 900/2,710 tons. Oil: 790 tons.
Endurance: 4,500 nm at 10 knots, coal only; 6,620 nm at 10 knots, coal and oil.
Armament: 10 x 12-inch; 16 x 4-inch (later 4 x 4-inch replaced by 2 x 3-inch AA); 4 x 3-pdr;
3 x 18-inch torpedo tubes.
Armour: Belt: 10 - 2½ inch; Deck: 3 - ¾ inch; Barbette: 10 - 5 inch; Turret and conning tower: 11 inch.
Complement: 813

She joined the 1st Battle Squadron in May 1912 and was still serving there in August 1914 when the squadron joined the Grand Fleet. On 18th March 1915 a U-boat made an unsuccessful attempt to torpedo her off the Pentland Firth while returning from exercises. This U-boat was then sunk by *Dreadnought*. At Jutland she engaged and hit *Lutzow*. Shortly after the battle, in June, she transferred to the 4th BS. She went into reserve in February 1919 and was sold for breaking up in September 1922.

*With an M class destroyer at the surrender of the German Fleet. Admiral Beatty was on the Admiral's Bridge watching the ships steam past to enter the Firth of Forth. Passing in the background here are the Konig class battleships **Grosser Kurfurst**, on the right, and **Markgraf** 21st November 1918.*

Queen Elizabeth Class Battleship

H.M. Dockyard, Portsmouth
Laid down: 21st October 1912; Launched: 16 October 1913; Completed: January 1915
Length: 639 ft 9 in.
Power: Four-shaft Parsons turbines; 75,000 shp - 24 knots. 24 Babcock and Wilcox boilers.
Complement: c. 1,100 as flagship

(For other class details, see *Barham* page 107)

Commissioned at Portsmouth on 22nd December 1914, she was first sent to the Mediterranean in February 1915 as Flagship, East Mediterranean Squadron, for the Dardanelles Campaign. She fired against the Narrows forts and in support of the landings from February to May. As a brand new ship of the most modern design she was withdrawn because of the danger from mines or U-boat attack. She struck Adm. de Robeck's flag and left for Gibraltar on 14th May and arrived at Scapa Flow on the 26th to join the 5th Battle Squadron. She was in refit at Rosyth from 22nd May to the 4th June 1916 and consequently was not present at Jutland. On her return she was temporary flagship, 5th BS and then started another refit in November which was completed in February 1917. This prepared her for recommissioning as Fleet Flagship for Admiral Beatty as C-in-C, Grand Fleet. She temporarily wore the flag of Adm. Mayo, United States Navy, on the 9-10th September 1917. On 15th November 1918 the Terms of Surrender of the German High Seas Fleet were signed on board. She was flagship, Atlantic Fleet, 1919 - 24, and then of the Mediterranean Fleet until 1926. She was partially modernized in 1926 - 27 and completely reconstructed in 1937 - 41. She served through the rest of the Second World War and went into reserve in August 1945. She was sold for breaking up in April 1948.

At peace in Weymouth Bay in 1919 having survived some severe maulings during the war. She has aircraft platforms on Q and Y turrets, the latter with a Sopwith Camel on the platform with the direction of take-off over the rear of the turret, rather than over the guns as in most capital ships, and as with her own platform on Q turret.

Lion Class Battlecruiser

H.M. Dockyard, Devonport
Laid down: 29th November 1909; Launched: 6th August 1910; Completed May 1912

(For class data notes, see *Princess Royal* page 51)

In June 1912 **Lion** joined the 1st Cruiser Squadron, becoming flagship from July. In March 1913 she was the flagship of Rear Admiral Beatty in the 1st Battlecruiser Squadron, joining the Grand Fleet in August 1914. In the Heligoland Bight action on 28th August, she sank the German cruiser *Ariadne*. On 24th January 1915, in the Dogger Bank battle, she scored hits on **Blucher**, **Derfflinger** and **Seydlitz**. The latter ship was severely damaged, both her aft turrets being burnt out, and she was only saved by the prompt flooding of the magazines – something that would have echoes for **Lion** seventeen months later. At Dogger Bank **Lion** was hit 17 times and seriously damaged with her engines disabled. She was towed home by **Indomitable**, receiving temporary repairs at Rosyth before being taken to the Tyne for permanent repairs. She returned to service in April 1915 as flagship of the newly constituted Battlecruiser Force. At Jutland she received further severe damage, being hit 13 times by **Lützow**. The worst was the hit on Q turret which blew the roof off, killing or wounding all in the gunhouse and igniting the cordite in the loading cages. The order given by Major F.J.W. Harvey, Royal Marine Light Infantry, (though mortally wounded with both legs blown off), to flood the magazines, saved the ship. Major Harvey was posthumously awarded the Victoria Cross. The turret was removed and **Lion** returned to service without it from 20th July to 23rd September. In November 1916 she became flagship for Rear Admiral Pakenham. In April 1919 she was in the Atlantic Fleet and in March 1920 went into reserve at Rosyth. She paid-off under the terms of the Washington Treaty in May 1922 and was sold for breaking up in January 1924.

Arriving at Gibraltar at 1700 on 24th February 1919 with Admiral Lord Jellicoe on board.

Indefatigable Class Battlecruiser

Fairfield Shipbuilding & Engineering Co.Ltd., Govan
Laid down: 20th June 1910; Launched: 1st July 1911; Completed: November 1912
Displacement: 18,750 tons (norm), 22,080 tons (full load)
Length: 590 ft 0 in; Beam: 80 ft 0 in; Draught: 24 ft 9 in (norm.), 27 ft 0 in (full load)
Power: Four-shaft Parsons turbines; 44,000 shp - 25 knots. 31 Babcock & Wilcox boilers.
Coal: 1,000/3,170 tons. Oil: 840 tons.
Endurance: 3,500 nm at 18 knots, 6,690 nm at 10 knots.
Armament: 8 x 12-inch; 16 x 4-inch; 4 x 3-pdr; 2 x 18-inch torpedo tubes.
Armour: Belt: 6 - 4 inch; Deck: 2½ - 1 inch; Turret: 7 inch; Barbette: 7 - 3 inch; Conning tower: 10 inch.
Complement: 806; 853 in 1919

She was built for the Government of the Dominion of New Zealand, but a lack of manpower and maintenance facilities meant that she was presented to the Royal Navy on completion. From January to December 1913 she went on a world cruise and visited New Zealand. On her return she joined the 1st Battlecruiser Squadron and at the outbreak of war transferred to the 2nd BCS and was at the Heligoland Bight action. In September 1914 she was back with the 1st BCS and then the 2nd BCS in January 1915 where she was, for a time, flagship. At Dogger Bank, Rear Admiral Moore took command when *Lion* was put out of action. She was refitted in April – May 1916 and was at Jutland. From June to November she was again with the 1st BCS then, at last, settled with the 2nd BCS until the end of the war. She was refitted between December 1918 and February 1919 in preparation for Admiral Lord Jellicoe's tour of the Dominions. She left Portsmouth on 21st February, her route including Gibraltar, Port Said, Suez, Bombay, Colombo, the Cocos Islands, Australia, Tasmania, New Zealand, Pacific Islands, Vancouver, San Diego and Caribbean Islands. On the west coast of North America, on 20th November, Jellicoe left the ship for an extensive rail-tour of Canada and United States and rejoined the ship at Key West on 8th January 1920. *New Zealand* arrived at Portsmouth on 3rd February having steamed 33,514 nautical miles. In March she went into reserve at Rosyth and was also listed for disposal under the Washington Treaty and sold for breaking up in December 1922.

In 1919, wearing her postwar pendant number.

Thornycroft M Class Destroyer

J.I. Thornycroft & Co.Ltd., Woolston
Laid down: September 1915; Launched: 26th August 1916; Completed: October 1916
Displacement: 1,033 tons.
Length: 274 ft 0 in; Beam: 27 ft 6 in; Draught: 10 ft 6 in.
Power: Three-shaft Brown-Curtis turbines; 27,500 shp - 35 knots. 3 Yarrow boilers. Oil: 254 tons.
Armament: 3 x 4-inch; 1 x 2-pdr; 4 x 21-inch torpedo tubes.
Complement: 80

Her wartime service with the Grand Fleet was, apparently, unremarkable but this photograph shows well the very different appearance of the destroyers built by the leading private constructors, Thornycroft and Yarrow, who were allowed considerable freedom in design, within the constraints of the requirements, rather than having to follow the standard. (Compare *Mystic* page 40). (This privilege was due to their experience with the type from the earliest days of development - *Havock* by Yarrow and *Daring* by Thornycroft, both launched in 1893, were the very first torpedo boat destroyers, evolved from the earlier, smaller, torpedo boats, development of which had started in the mid - 1870s). *Ready* went to the breakers in July 1926.

Hunt Class Minesweeper

Ailsa Shipbuilding Co.Ltd., Troon and Ayr
Launched: 8th March 1917; Completed: June 1917
Displacement: 750 tons.
Length: 231 ft 0 in; Beam: 28 ft 0 in; Draught: 7 ft 0 in.
Power: Two-shaft, three-cylinder triple expansion engines; 1,800 ihp - 16 knots. 2 Yarrow boilers.
Coal: 140 tons.
Armament: 1 x 12-pdr; 1 x 6-pdr; (later ships had two of each).
Complement: 71

This class was designed by Ailsa to improve on the paddle minesweepers. Experience had shown that the latter ships ran the risk of fouling moored mines with their paddles; an additional drawback was their poor performance in bad weather when, as they rolled, one or other of the paddles would come out of the water, leading to reduced speed and erratic steering. As minesweeping at that time was carried out in pairs, with the sweep connected to both ships, this was a considerable disadvantage (The single-ship sweep, later known as the Oropesa sweep, did not begin to come into service until the last year of the war). *Belvoir* was one of the first group, ordered in mid-1916, and despite the general class name, these were the only ones to be named after Hunts. Later orders were given names of towns throughout the British Isles. She joined the 3rd Fleet Sweeping Flotilla at Granton. She was sold for breaking up in July 1922.

In 1919; her flying-off platforms on B and Q turrets are in the process of being removed. In fact, though fitted, she had never carried any aircraft.

Iron Duke Class Battleship

H.M. Dockyard, Devonport
Laid down: 25th January 1912; Launched: 24th October 1912; Completed: June 1914
Displacement: 26,100 tons (norm.), 31,400 tons (deep load)
Length: 623 ft 0 in; Beam: 90 ft 1 in; Draught: 28 ft 8 in (norm.), 29 ft 6 in (deep)
Power: Four-shaft Parsons turbines; 29,000 shp - 21 knots. 18 Yarrow boilers.
Coal: 900 tons (min.), 3,250 tons (max.). Oil: 1,050 tons plus 550 tons in emergency tanks.
Endurance: 7,780 nm at 10 knots; 8,100 nm at 12 knots on coal and oil.
Armament: 10 x 13.5-inch; 12 x 6-inch; 2 x 3-inch AA; 4 x 3-pdr; 4 x 21-inch torpedo tubes.
Armour: Belt: 12 - 4 inch; Deck: 2½ - 1 inch; Barbette: 10 - 3 inch; Turret and Conning tower: 11 inch.
Complement: 925, 1,180 in 1918

In June 1914 she joined the Home Fleet as flagship of the 1st Battle Squadron and second flagship of the Fleet; and, in August, 1st BS became part of the Grand Fleet. At Jutland, on 1st June 1916, she was hit by a single torpedo from an unknown assailant. The hit, on the starboard side amidships, opened a 70 x 20 foot hole in the side plating next to the coal bunkers. Despite flooding, she maintained her station at 17 knots and only stopped firing when her list prevented the guns from bearing. She avoided three further torpedoes from German destroyers and reduced speed to avoid straining her bulkheads. She made her way home at 10 knots with her draught increased to 39 feet (some 10 feet greater than normal) and came under attack by a U-boat which failed. She reached safety in the Humber at 1900 on 2nd June and was taken to the Tyne for repairs which lasted two months. She was the only Dreadnought in the Royal Navy to be torpedoed in the war. Postwar, she went with the rest of the class to the Mediterranean where she remained, apart from a refitting period, until 1926. She then came home and was in the Atlantic Fleet until 1931; in June that year she paid-off and was used in explosive and aerial bombing experiments until May 1932 and was sold for breaking up in June.

Laid up in the River Tamar, upstream of Brunel's Saltash railway bridge, in 1920. She was sold for scrapping to Marple and Gillott of Saltash on 29th November 1921.

Acorn Class Destroyer

John Brown & Co. Ltd., Clydebank
Laid down: 12th January 1910; Launched: 1st July 1910; Completed: December 1910.

(For class data notes, see ***Sheldrake*** page 65)

Acorn's war service matched that of her sister ***Sheldrake***, starting in 1914 with 2nd Destroyer Flotilla, Grand Fleet and then going out to the Mediterranean until war's end.

Preserved where she was built at Thornycroft's boatyard on Platt's Eyot on the River Thames, near Hampton. 26th October 1964.

40-Foot Class Coastal Motor Boat

Displacement: 5 tons.
Length: 45 ft 0 in; Beam: 8ft 6 in; Draught: 2ft 6 in. to 3 ft 0 in.
Power: Single-shaft, Thornycroft V8 or V12 petrol engine; 250 bhp - 24.8 knots.
Armament: 1 x 18-inch torpedo; 2 to 4 x Lewis machine guns.
Crew of two or three

The Coastal Motor Boats were the pioneers in the development of naval, wooden-construction, high-speed planing boats for making attacks with torpedoes. The design was based on Thornycroft's pre-war experience with racing hydroplanes and after discussions with naval officers as to requirements. The first twelve were ordered in January 1916 and all delivered by mid-August. The method of operation was for the boat to be driven at full speed towards the target, the torpedo, in a trough in the after part of the boat, would be fired, tail first, over the stern and the boat immediately turned away to allow the torpedo to run straight ahead. It was intended that the boats could be hoisted onboard by cruisers' davits to carry them to within striking distance of any target but this was never put into practice as the most likely targets were close to Britain across the North Sea and the boats could operate directly from ports or be towed to a starting position by destroyers. On 8th April 1917 *CMB 4* led one of the few successful attacks by those craft when she, with *CMBs 5*, *6* and *9* skimmed over the minefields and fired torpedoes at four destroyers off Zeebrugge. *CMB 4*'s torpedo missed but two of the others' hit and sank *G88*. *CMB 4*'s greatest claim to fame, however, began when a secret base was opened on Osea Island, in the River Blackwater in Essex, commandeered in 1917. Here a flotilla was formed for a planned attack on the German High Seas Fleet in the Baltic but the war ended before it could be carried out. Postwar involvement of the Royal Navy in the supporting of the independent Baltic states against Bolshevik forces meant that the training experience of the CMB crews could be put to use after all. A plan was prepared for two CMBs to be taken to the Gulf of Finland to pick up a British agent from Petrograd – in the event this never happened and the agent eventually crossed into Finland on foot. However, a new plan was made to attack the Bolshevik island naval base at Kronstadt in the approaches to Petrograd. From the tiny Finnish harbour at Terrioki, close to the Russian border, *CMB 4* set off on the night of 16/17th June 1919 to attack the armoured cruiser *Oleg* which had been bombarding the White Russian-held fort at Krasnaya Gorka, on the mainland to the south. Just past midnight, *CMB 4* fired her torpedo amidst intense defensive fire from the cruiser and accompanying destroyers. The torpedo hit amidships and *Oleg* quickly heeled over and sank. Eight CMBs (not *CMB 4*) set out to attack Kronstadt harbour on the 18th August, inflicting considerable damage on ships present there. Awards to the crew of *CMB 4* for the *Oleg* attack were – to Lt. Augustus Agar, the Victoria Cross; Sub.Lt. John Hampsheir, the Distinguished Service Cross and Chief Motor Mechanic Hugh Beeley, the Conspicuous Gallantry Medal. Once returned to Britain, *CMB 4* was displayed at the Motor Boat Exhibition at Olympia, in London, in 1920. From 1921 to 1928 she was lent to the Imperial War Museum and then preserved at Platt's Eyot. Subsequently, after years of deterioration and being moved from site to site, her, sadly, gutted hull was restored and is now with the IWM collection at Duxford.

Also laid up in the Tamar in 1920

24 Class Fleet Sweeping Sloop

Greenock & Grangemouth Dockyard Co.
Launched: 27th April 1918
Displacement: 1,320 tons
Length: 267 ft 6 in; Beam: 35 ft 0 in; Draught: 10 ft 6 in.
Power: Single-shaft, triple expansion engine; 2500 ihp - 17 knots. 2 boilers.
Coal: 260 tons. Endurance: 3,000 naut.miles at 12 ½ knots.
Armament: 2 x 4-inch; 39 depth charges.
Complement: 82

This sloop type followed the Flower class and was of similar dimensions; however, their appearance was completely different as it was intended as a variation on the decoy theme. They purported to be 'double-ended' in profile with matching deckhouses and gunshields forward and aft. It is clear though, from this photograph, that the hull lines were normal, that is with flared bow and conventional stern, the latter ending at a vertical sternpost. The bridge was also not mirrored exactly by the aft cylindrical deckhouse – however her dazzle-paint scheme went to the extent of providing an 'anchor' at the stern; They proved to be poor seaboats, given to rolling, and were not liked as well as the Flowers. Twenty-four ships were ordered and the class was thus known simply as the '24' class. This was because their names, of famous racehorses, would normally have made them the Racehorse class, but this would have caused confusion with the Racecourse class paddle minesweepers. As they appeared late in the war, only 22 ships were, in fact, completed. (Donovan was the 1889 Derby winner). The ship was sold to breakers in November 1922.

HMS Sceptre (H79)

Alexander Stephen & Sons Ltd., Linthouse, Govan
Laid down: 10th November 1915; Launched: 18th April 1917; Completed: May 1917

Sold to breakers: December 1926.

HMS Tetrarch (G55)

Harland & Wolff, Govan
Laid down: 26th July 1916; Launched: 20th April 1917; Completed: June 1917

Sold to breakers: July 1934.

*Both photographs (**Tetrarch** overleaf) date from circa 1920/21.*

To conclude, a last look at a pair of the Royal Navy's workhorses - the destroyers. Most of the Admiralty R class were in service with the Grand Fleet destroyer flotillas or with the Harwich Force, carrying out the endless duty of routine patrols looking for enemy surface forces or submarines returning to base, and most often, by 1917 and to the end of the war, finding nothing but rough weather and 'Hard Lying'. Once the war was over, the R class survivors continued to serve, whereas many of the earlier destroyers, all those built pre-war and the

majority of the M class, were laid up prior to disposal. Of the 39 Admiralty Rs built, five were lost (three mined, one torpedoed and one in a collision). The other 34 served on into the 1920s but all but ten of these were sold between 1926 and 1929. The others sailed on doing useful training tasks until, by the end of 1937, only one was left. This was **Skate** (John Brown, launched 11th January 1917) which was attached to the Torpedo School at Portsmouth. When war began again she returned to active service as one of the vital, but scarce in the early days, escorts. She was, in fact, the oldest Royal Navy destroyer in the Second World War (including all the ex-American four-stackers). Fitted with radar, and with her second and third funnels reduced in height, she was unique in appearance and looked elegant in the Peter Scott Western Approaches camouflage. During an escort duty, when her identity was challenged with the question " What ship is that?", she flashed the immortal reply "Churchill's Secret Weapon".....

APPENDIX

ROYAL NAVY WARSHIP LOSSES
4 AUGUST 1914 - 11 NOVEMBER 1918
12 NOVEMBER 1918 - 31 DECEMBER 1919

The following tables sum up the total losses of vessels in Royal Naval service during the war. Note particularly the high number of losses to that fearsome weapon, the mine; the increasing threat of the submarine and the number of accidental losses.

Key:

Types		Causes	
AC	Armoured Cruiser	a	Mine
AM	Armed Merchant Cruiser/ Commissioned	b	Torpedo, submarine
	Escort Ship/ Armed Boarding Steamer	c	Torpedo, surface
AMS	Admiralty Minesweeper	d	Gunfire, naval
AT	Admiralty Trawler	e	Gunfire, shore
AUX	Miscellaneous Auxiliary	f	Aircraft bombs or machine-gun fire
B	Battleship	g	Rammed U-boat and sank
BC	Battlecruiser	h	Captured by enemy
C	Cruiser	i	Scuttled by enemy
CMB	Coastal Motor Boat	j	Collision and sunk
D	Destroyer	k	Run aground and wrecked
HD	Hired Drifter	l	Sprang a leak and sank
HMS	Hired Paddle or Screw Minesweeper	m	Stress of weather
HT	Hired Trawler	n	Internal explosion
M	Monitor	o	Accidental fire
ML	Motor Launch	p	Destroyed by crew to prevent capture
MLR	Minelayer	q	Expended/scuttled by explosives
O	Oiler	r	Cause unknown
PB	Pre-Dreadnought Battleship		
PBO	P-Boat		
Q	Decoy/Q Ship		
S	Submarine		
SC	Seaplane Carrier		
TB	Torpedo Boat		

With due acknowledgement to those invaluable books:

British Warships 1914-1919; F.J. Dittmar & J.J. Colledge; Ian Allan, 1972
British Warship Losses in the Ironclad Era 1860-1919; David Hepper; Chatham Publishing, 2006

1914

TYPE	CAUSE a	b	c	d	e	f	g	h	i	j	k	l	m	n	o	p	q	r	Total
B	1																		1
PB														1					1
AC		3		2															5
C	1	2		1															4
D											1								1
S	1	1																2	4
SC		1																	1
AMS	1	1																	2
AT											1								1
HT	8										4								12
HD	2																		2
AM											1								1
AUX													1						1
TOTAL	14	8		3							7		1	1				2	36

1915

TYPE	CAUSE a	b	c	d	e	f	g	h	i	j	k	l	m	n	o	p	q	r	Total
PB	1	3	1		1														6
AC											1			1					2
D	4	1									3								8
S	3	1		2	1											1		2	10
TB	2									1	1		1						5
MLR														1					1
AT	2																		2
HT	25	1	1							12	10								49
HD	3			2						3	2		2					1	13
HMS	3									1			1						5
AM		3	1										1					1	6
AUX	2			4	2					2	3		2		5				20
TOTAL	45	9	3	8	4					19	20		7	2	5	1		4	127

1916	CAUSE																		
	a	b	c	d	e	f	g	h	i	j	k	l	m	n	o	p	q	r	
PB	2																		2
BC				3															3
AC	1			3															4
C	1	2																	3
M					1														1
D	1	1	1	6						6									15
S	8	1				1					2								12
TB	1									2									3
AMS	3	2	1																6
AT	1										1								2
HT	36	1		6						5	6	2	2						58
HD	16			11		1				7	6								41
HMS		1																	1
AM	1	1		1															3
Q		2								1									3
ML		3													3				6
AUX	6	1		1				1		1	2	1							13
TOTAL	77	15	2	31	1	2		1		22	17	3	2		3				176

1917	Cause																		
Type \	a	b	c	d	e	f	g	h	i	j	k	l	m	n	o	p	q	r	
B														1					1
PB		1																	1
AC		1																	1
M		1																	1
D	9	5	3	2						4									23
S	1	1								3						1		1	7
SC					1														1
TB										1	1								2
PBO	1																		1
MLR		1																	1
AMS	6	4																1	11
AT	1	1		1					1										4
HT	59	6		5					1	9	6							2	88
HD	13			15						5	3	1	1		3				41
HMS	3	1								1									5
AM	1	9									1		1						12
Q		13		4						1						1			19
ML		2									2				3				7
CMB				1						1						1			3
O		3																	3
AUX	5	2								1	2								10
Total	99	51	3	28	1				2	26	15	1	2	1	6	3		4	242

1918 / TYPE	CAUSE																		
	a	b	c	d	e	f	g	h	i	j	k	l	m	n	o	p	q	r	
PB		1																	1
C																	6		6
M	1			2							1			1					5
D	3	3			1		1			7	4								19
S	1	1		2	1	1				3						7	1	4	21
SC										1									1
TB													1						1
PBO										1									1
AMS	3	4								1									8
AT		1		1						5									7
HT	16	4		2						11	2	2			1				38
HD	6	1		7						17	1	1			1				34
HMS	1																		1
AM		9									1								10
Q		2		2							1	1			1				7
ML	1	1			3						2				3				10
CMB						6		1		1					3	1		1	13
O		2																	2
AUX	1	5		1					2	3	7		2						21
TOTAL	33	34		17	5	7	1	1	2	50	19	4	3	1	9	8	7	5	206

1918-1919		CAUSE																		
		a	b	c	d	e	f	g	h	i	j	k	l	m	n	o	p	q	r	
TYPE	AC											1									1
	C	1																			1
	M																	2			2
	D	1	1									1									3
	S	1										1									2
	AMS	7																			7
	HT	1										1									2
	HD	1										1	2								4
	HMS	2																			2
	ML										2	3		2							7
	CMB				2							1		2				4			9
	AUX	1									1	5		1				2			10
	TOTAL	15	1		2						3	14	2	5				8			50

*The 2nd Light Cruiser Squadron in the North Sea in late 1917 or early 1918. The leader, **Birmingham**, has her kite balloon up; second in the line is **Dublin** followed by **Melbourne** and the photograph is taken from either **Sydney** or **Southampton**, depending on the exact date.*

INDEX